Earth is BIG

Written by **STEVE TOMECEK**

Illustrated by **MARCOS FARINA**

What on Earth Books

CONTENTS

INTRODUCTION

The Earth is our home, the only place we humans have ever lived and for most of our history the only place we knew existed. But once we began to study outer space, we also started to discover that our planet is just one of many in the universe. Since then, we have ventured out into space and looked back at Earth from afar, like a big blue ball in a sea of black. The images from space have made us keenly aware of something: as big as Earth seems to us here on the surface, our planet is really tiny compared to the vastness of space!

Even so, our home planet is quite different from the rest of the known worlds in our solar system. Over billions of years, different processes have shaped and molded it into a home like no other. One of the best ways to get a better understanding of our home sweet home, is to find out how Earth—and the things that live on it—compare to the rest of the universe! That's what this book is all about.

The best way to compare two things is to measure them. We humans like to measure things. There's something powerful about knowing how big, how heavy, or how fast something is and being able to compare a tortoise to a cheetah to a race car to a comet. Once you get started measuring and comparing, you'll notice we do it all the time. We measure the temperature outside on a warm summer day, the pressure of the air in a perfectly inflated soccer ball, and our own ages so we can compare them to the ages of our friends and family.

Measuring and comparing also lets you see things from different angles. Our planet orbits the Sun at an average distance of about 93 million miles (150 million kilometers). Is that far? Well, it depends what you compare it to. It's a lot farther than a snail can walk in an hour or even a lifetime, but it's much closer than Pluto.

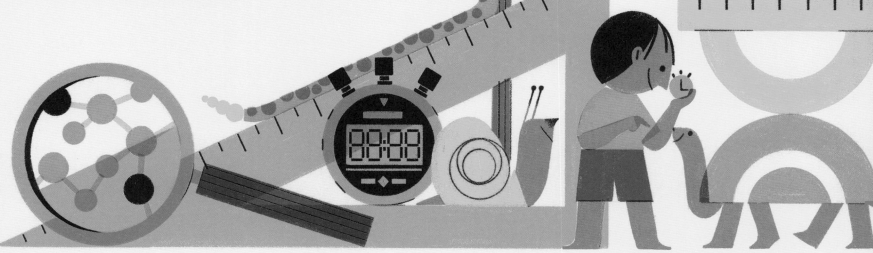

Is the Earth heavy? Well, yes. It has a mass of approximately 6.6 sextillion tons (6 septillion kilograms). That's a 6 with 21 zeros after it! That seems like an awful lot, doesn't it? But when you look at how dense the Earth is, how much mass fits in each bit of space, all of a sudden Earth starts to look pretty light. There are a lot of metals that are denser than Earth, including familiar ones like iron and silver and gold.

In this book we explore our planet (and a lot of other things) through measurement and comparison. To do that, we use what are known as standards of measurement, units we have all agreed to, such as feet, pounds, meters, kilograms, tons, and degrees. This agreement is key. If we were to measure distance, for example, by the number of steps it takes to travel it, then my measurement and yours would be different because we take different-sized steps. That's why people invented standard units. Throughout this book, we'll explore a lot of different standards. Some will be very familiar to you. Others might be totally new. But all of them are fun because they give you the power to understand the world around us.

So welcome to big, small, heavy, light, cold, hot, wet, dry, fast, slow, round, jagged planet Earth, a fantastic home by any measure!

A note on the measurements in this book

Across the globe, there are lots of different systems for measuring things. But, wherever you are, scientists use what's called the metric system, and many countries do too. The metric system uses standard units such as meters and kilograms for their measurements. In this book you'll see both United States customary units and metric units. Information on converting metric to United States customary units, such as inches and pounds, can be found on page 43 of this book.

EARTH IS BIG

How big is the Earth? The most common way of measuring the size of a planet is to use its diameter, which is the distance from one edge to another running through the center at the equator. Earth's diameter is 7,926 miles (12,756 kilometers). Let's see how some smaller objects compare.

THE SOLAR SYSTEM

Our solar system contains planets, moons, and lots of smaller objects. Some, including planets and dwarf planets, orbit the Sun. Moons orbit planets. Many of these objects are smaller than Earth, including Earth's Moon, our closest neighbor in space.

EARTH
7,926 miles
(12,756 km)
Our planet

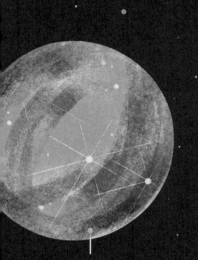

MERCURY
3,032 miles
(4,879 km)
Smallest planet and closest planet to the Sun

EARTH'S MOON
2,159 miles
(3,475 km)
Fifth-largest moon in the solar system • When you compare the size of the Moon to the size of the Earth, it is the largest moon compared to the size of the planet it orbits (excluding dwarf planets).

CERES
592 miles
(952 km)
Dwarf planet

PLUTO
1,473 miles
(2,370 km)
Dwarf planet • When it was first discovered in 1930, Pluto was labelled as the ninth planet in the solar system. But as scientists discovered more objects in space, Pluto became one of the first of a new group of objects called dwarf planets instead.

VENUS
7,521 miles
(12,104 km)

CHARON
750 miles
(1,207 km)
Largest of Pluto's moons

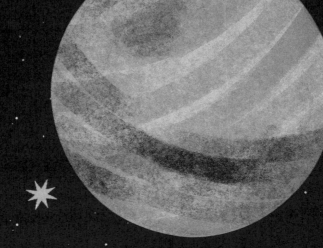

MARS
4,220 miles
(6,792 km)

HOW BIG IS BIG?

Miles and kilometers

When people want to know how wide, high, or long something is, they use units of length. In the metric system, the standard unit of length is the meter. We measure large distances in miles or kilometers (km). 1 km equals 1,000 meters, or 3,281 ft, or 0.62 miles.

LONGEST NONSTOP COMMERCIAL FLIGHT
9,534 miles
(15,343 km)

AMAZON RIVER
4,000 miles
(6,437 km)

GREAT WALL OF CHINA
13,170 miles (21,196 km)

Feet, inches, and meters

Feet, inches and meters can be used for measuring everyday objects and creatures, including the length or height of large animals such as humans.

CAPYBARA
4 ft 3 in
(1.3 m)
Largest rodent

Coming up with a height for an "average human" is not easy because in some parts of the world people are naturally taller than in other places.

HUMAN
8 ft 11 in
(2.72 m)
Tallest person ever

BLUE WHALE
98 ft
(30 m)
Largest animal

GIRAFFE
18 ft
(5.5 m)
Tallest land animal

Inches and millimeters

For small objects, inches can be used, or the meter can be divided into centimeters (cm) or millimeters (mm). One hundred centimeters make up a meter, and one thousand millimeters make up a meter.

LADYBUG
0.2 in
(5 mm)

BUMBLEBEE BAT
1.2 in
(30 mm)
Smallest mammal • The tiny bumblebee bat is found in Thailand and Myanmar.

PINHEAD
0.03 in
(1 mm)

GIANT HUNTSMAN
12 in
(300 mm)
Largest spider by leg span

Microns

Even smaller objects can be measured in microns. There are one million microns in a meter, or 304,800 in a foot. All of these objects are too small for the human eye to see without a microscope.

RED BLOOD CELL
6–8 microns
Most common cell in the human body
All living things, from giant redwood trees to tiny bacteria swimming in pond water, are made from different types of cells. Scientists estimate that you have more than 30 trillion cells in your body.

LACTOBACILLUS ACIDOPHILUS
2–9 microns
Helpful bacteria found in the gut
Bacteria are microscopic, single-celled organisms. They live in every type of environment, including our bodies. Some cause diseases, while others can be helpful.

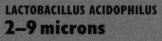

CORONAVIRUS
0.12 microns
Even smaller than bacteria, many viruses attack cells and take them over, causing you to become sick. One type of coronavirus caused a global pandemic in 2020 and 2021.

Nanometers

Extremely small objects are measured in nanometers. There are one billion nanometers in a meter, or 304,800,000 in a foot. These objects require high tech equipment, such as an electron microscope, to "see" them.

CESIUM ATOM
0.26 nanometers
Largest naturally ocurring atom • Everything from the air you breathe to your body's cells is made of tiny building blocks called atoms. At the heart of an atom is the nucleus. This is made up of smaller particles called protons and, usually, neutrons. Whizzing around it are even smaller particles called electrons. Different atoms contain different numbers of these particles.

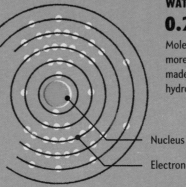

— Nucleus
— Electron

WATER MOLECULE
0.27 nanometers
Molecules are made up of two or more atoms. Water molecules are made from one oxygen and two hydrogen atoms.

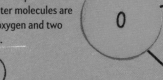

HYDROGEN ATOM
0.05 nanometers
Smallest atom

EARTH IS SMALL

From Earth, our planet can seem really big. But when you compare Earth's diameter with some of the other objects in space, such as the gas giant planets, it turns out that our planet's really not that big at all. Here are some examples of different sized objects in the solar system and even further out in space.

EARTH
7,926 miles
(12,756 km)

URANUS
31,763 miles
(51,118 km)

GIANT PLANETS OF THE SOLAR SYSTEM

Mercury, Venus, Earth, and Mars are the closest planets to the Sun. They are mostly made of rock and metal and are small and dense. But the four outer planets, Jupiter, Saturn, Uranus, and Neptune, are made mostly of condensed gases and are all much larger than Earth.

JUPITER
88,846 miles (142,984 km)

Largest planet in the solar system • Jupiter's diameter is about 11 times Earth's. Almost 200 years ago, astronomers spotted a giant oval-shaped storm on the planet called the Great Red Spot. It's still raging and, at more than 9,941 miles (16,000 km) wide, is large enough to swallow up the entire Earth!

NEPTUNE
30,775 miles
(49,528 km)

LET THERE BE LIGHT-YEARS

OUR SOLAR SYSTEM

4.2 light-years

PROXIMA CENTAURI

For measuring distances on Earth, units such as meters and kilometers work fine. But in space you'll run into a problem: there's a lot of empty space in space! Take Proxima Centauri. After the Sun it's the next closest star to Earth. It's over 24,000,000,000,000 (that's 24 trillion) miles away (40 trillion km)!

To deal with these enormous distances, scientists use a unit of measurement called a light-year. One light-year is the distance that a beam of light travels in one year, about 5.88 trillion miles (9.46 trillion km). That means Proxima Centauri is about 4.2 light-years away.

SATURN
74,898 miles
(120,536 km)

Ringed gas giant • The most famous feature of Saturn is the rings circling the planet. Made mostly of tiny bits of ice and rock, the rings are about 167,770 miles (270,000 km) wide when measured from one edge to the other.

STAR LIGHT, STAR BRIGHT

Every star that you can see with your naked eye is much bigger than the Earth. The reason they all look so small is because they are very far away from us. Even though it looks much larger than the rest of the stars that we see at night, the Sun is only a medium-sized star.

BETELGEUSE
870 million miles
(1.4 billion km)

109,752 times wider than Earth
Betelgeuse is one of the biggest stars that astronomers know of. It can be seen shining brightly on the shoulder of the constellation Orion.

JUPITER
88,846 miles
(142,984 km)

EARTH
7,926 miles
(12,756 km)

THE SUN
864,337 miles
(1.39 million km)
109 times wider than Earth

SIRIUS B
1.5 million miles
(2.4 million km)
188 times wider than Earth

ONE GREAT GALAXY

Our Sun does not travel through space alone. It is part of a huge group of stars called the Milky Way Galaxy that is being held together by the force of gravity. If you could get way out into space and look back at our galaxy, you would see that it looks like a giant, slowly turning pinwheel. Astronomers still aren't sure how many stars there are in the Milky Way Galaxy, but the current estimate is somewhere between 100 and 400 billion!

The closest galaxy to our own is the Andromeda Galaxy. It is "only" around 2.5 million light-years from Earth.

MILKY WAY GALAXY
About 100,000 light-years across
Our galaxy

ANDROMEDA GALAXY
200,000 light-years across
Our closest neighbor

Location of solar system in the Milky Way

OUR GALACTIC NEIGHBORHOOD

Our Milky Way is only one of the billions of galaxies that astronomers have identified in space! These galaxies are usually found in clumps held together by the force of gravity. The clump of galaxies that the Milky Way belongs to is called the Local Group. Astronomers estimate that there may be more than 30 individual galaxies in the Local Group.

The Local Group cluster is part of an even bigger group called the Virgo Supercluster. This enormous structure contains over a million galaxies.

MILK WAY GALAXY
About 100,000 light-years across

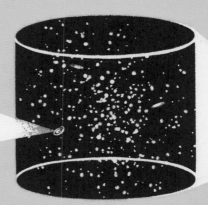

LOCAL GROUP OF GALAXIES
10 million light-years across

VIRGO SUPERCLUSTER
110 million light-years across

EARTH IS OLD

Most scientists believe that our Earth formed roughly 4,540,000,000 (4.54 billion) years ago, give or take 50 million years. That's when a big swirling mass of gas and dust began to pull itself together under the force of gravity. The big clumps formed the Sun and planets of the solar system. Others became dwarf planets or asteroids. Here's how Earth has changed since it first formed.

EARTH FORMS
When Earth first formed it was bombarded by asteroids and comets. The surface was a molten mass of super-hot lava, which eventually cooled to form the solid crust of the planet we know today.

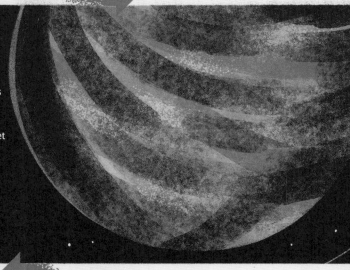

541 million years ago

CAMBRIAN EXPLOSION
For the first few billion years of Earth's history, life was very simple. It was mostly made up of single-celled organisms such as bacteria and, at the very end of the period, some life forms like nothing on Earth today. The first animals we might recognize—including sponges, mollusks, jellyfish, and trilobites—all appeared about the same time during the Cambrian period. This time is often called the Cambrian explosion.

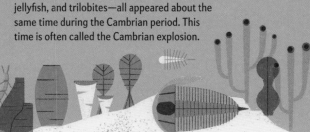

3.5 billion years ago

CYANOBACTERIA DEVELOP
One of the hottest debates among scientists is about when life first appeared on Earth. Some of the oldest possible evidence for living things are from hematite tubes that could have been made by ancient bacteria. But more well-understood fossils come from a type of simple life form called cyanobacteria. These are the earliest confirmed signs of life that scientists can agree on.

470 million years ago

PLANTS TAKE OVER THE LAND
The first plants grew in wetland environments. Known as *liverworts*, these simple plants still have relatives living today.

250 million years ago

MAMMALS
Humans belong to a group of animals called mammals. The ancestors of mammals split off from reptiles around this time. Early mammals lived side by side with the dinosaurs. Most early mammals were quite small, about the size of modern-day mice or squirrels. It wasn't until after the dinosaurs went extinct that mammals came to dominate the world.

TIME MARCHES ON
We use several different units to measure time. Two important units are the day and year, which are both based on the movement of the Earth. A day is defined as the length of time it takes for Earth to complete one full rotation, or spin around once, on its axis. A year is defined as the amount of time that it takes for the Earth to complete one orbit around the Sun. It takes 365.25 days for the Earth to orbit the Sun.

1 rotation = 1 day

1 orbit = 1 year

NOW

TODAY'S HUMANS
Humans continue to change and evolve even today. Can you imagine where we will be in another million years?

300,000 years ago

MODERN HUMANS
Modern humans (called *Homo sapiens*) have only been around for about 300,000 years. The first *Homo sapiens* lived in Africa, but our ancestors had probably spread around the world by about 70,000 years ago.

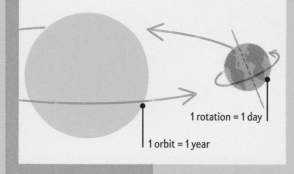

4.51 billion years ago

THE MOON FORMS

Most scientists believe that the Moon is only a little bit younger than Earth. The current theory is that the Moon formed when an object roughly the size of Mars, called Theia, slammed into the young Earth. Gravity pulled together the leftover debris to form the Moon.

4.4 billion years ago

ZIRCON CRYSTALS FORM

These minerals from the Jack Hills of Australia are the oldest known on Earth.

Zircon crystal

4.3 billion years ago

LIQUID WATER FORMS

As Earth cooled and the first rocks formed, a huge amount of a gas called water vapor was released into the atmosphere. Eventually, the water vapor cooled enough to become liquid water and begin filling the oceans.

4.2 billion years ago

HEMATITE TUBES FORM

Hematite tubes are possibly the first signs of life on Earth.

Crystal containing hematite tubes

Close-up of hematite tubes

4.28 billion years ago

NUVVUAGITTUQ GREENSTONE BELT

The oldest Earth rocks found so far come from this rock formation in Canada that was originally formed by a volcano but later changed. The metamorphic rocks are thought to be a leftover chunk of Earth's earliest oceanic crust.

240 million years ago

DINOSAURS

The first dinosaurs made their appearance around this time. Over the next 175 million years, this large group of animals would evolve to include gentle giants such as *Alamosaurus*, fearsome *Tyrannosaurus rex*, and many smaller critters too.

But their rule came to a sudden end roughly 65.5 million years ago when a large asteroid struck the Earth. The impact helped to create a climate catastrophe that caused all of the non-avian dinosaurs to go extinct.

130 million years ago

BIRDS

Most paleontologists believe that today's birds evolved from a group of dinosaurs called theropods. Many of these dinosaurs had feathers covering their bodies. Fossils of one early bird ancestor come from China. It's called *Archaeornithura* and is over 130 million years old.

2.4 million years ago

"HANDY MAN"

One early species of human is called *Homo habilis*. They lived in Africa between 2.4 and 1.4 million years ago. Standing about 1.37 m tall, *Homo habilis* had a bigger brain than earlier species and was an active tool maker. In fact, its name *Homo habilis* is Latin for "handy man."

4.4 million years ago

HUMAN ANCESTORS

Humans are relative newcomers on Earth. There is still a major debate among scientists about who the first true human ancestor is. One problem is that new fossils are being found all the time. Each one adds to the story.

One of the earliest human ancestors is called *Ardipithecus ramidus*. Nicknamed "Ardi," it is about 4.4 million years old. At first glance, it is far more ape-like than later humans. But the remains clearly belong to a creature that walked upright, just like us, separating it from other apes.

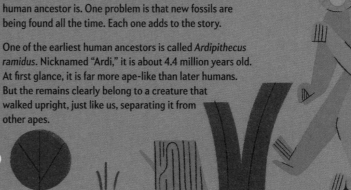

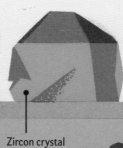

EARTH'S INHABITANTS ARE YOUNG

Compared to the billions of years the Earth has existed, the life of any individual living on it is very, very short. Trees have some of the longest lives of any plant or animal. Insects have some of the shortest. Humans are somewhere in between, with a maximum life span of about 122 years.

LIFE SPAN OR LIFE EXPECTANCY?

All living things have their own life span, which is the maximum length of time that members of a particular species can survive. The human life span is 122 years but, because of illness, accidents, and several other factors, most people don't live that long. The number that measures how long a person will probably actually live is called life expectancy. Today, the global average for a human is around 72 years.

JEANNE CALMENT
122 years, 164 days
This woman from France holds the record for longest-living person. She died in 1997.

INTO THE WOODS
Some trees can reach more than 5,000 years old—that's older than the Great Pyramid in Egypt.

GENERAL SHERMAN
2,500 years
A giant sequoia tree growing in California, named General Sherman, is believed to be the largest living tree on Earth. It's still growing.

BRISTLECONE PINE TREE
4,850 years
These ancient trees grow high up in the Rocky Mountains.

OAK TREE
1,000 years
Many common trees, including oaks, maples, and pines, have life spans of hundreds or even thousands of years.

OLD TJIKKO
9,500 years
Found in Sweden, the roots of this Norway spruce tree are almost 10,000 years old.

AGE INCREASES ACROSS THE SCALE FROM LEFT TO RIGHT

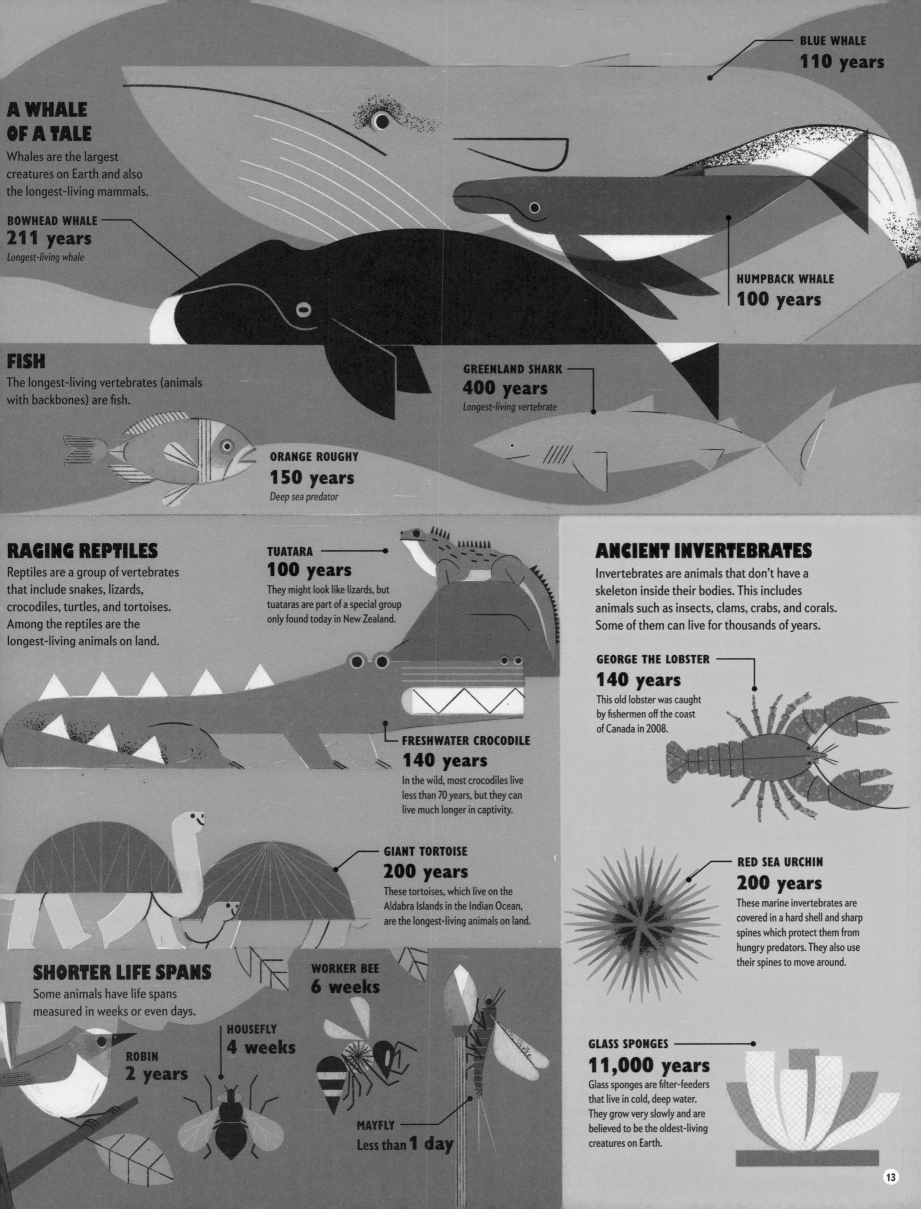

A WHALE OF A TALE

Whales are the largest creatures on Earth and also the longest-living mammals.

BOWHEAD WHALE
211 years
Longest-living whale

BLUE WHALE
110 years

HUMPBACK WHALE
100 years

FISH

The longest-living vertebrates (animals with backbones) are fish.

GREENLAND SHARK
400 years
Longest-living vertebrate

ORANGE ROUGHY
150 years
Deep sea predator

RAGING REPTILES

Reptiles are a group of vertebrates that include snakes, lizards, crocodiles, turtles, and tortoises. Among the reptiles are the longest-living animals on land.

TUATARA
100 years
They might look like lizards, but tuataras are part of a special group only found today in New Zealand.

FRESHWATER CROCODILE
140 years
In the wild, most crocodiles live less than 70 years, but they can live much longer in captivity.

GIANT TORTOISE
200 years
These tortoises, which live on the Aldabra Islands in the Indian Ocean, are the longest-living animals on land.

ANCIENT INVERTEBRATES

Invertebrates are animals that don't have a skeleton inside their bodies. This includes animals such as insects, clams, crabs, and corals. Some of them can live for thousands of years.

GEORGE THE LOBSTER
140 years
This old lobster was caught by fishermen off the coast of Canada in 2008.

RED SEA URCHIN
200 years
These marine invertebrates are covered in a hard shell and sharp spines which protect them from hungry predators. They also use their spines to move around.

SHORTER LIFE SPANS

Some animals have life spans measured in weeks or even days.

ROBIN
2 years

HOUSEFLY
4 weeks

WORKER BEE
6 weeks

MAYFLY
Less than **1 day**

GLASS SPONGES
11,000 years
Glass sponges are filter-feeders that live in cold, deep water. They grow very slowly and are believed to be the oldest-living creatures on Earth.

EARTH IS COLD

One of the main reasons that Earth is teeming with life is because of the planet's temperature. On the surface, Earth's temperature averages about 15 degrees Celsius (59°F). But that's just the average. Some places are a lot colder!

North Pole
(in winter)

Direct
sunlight

Equator

South Pole
(in summer)

CHILLIN' ON THE SURFACE

Because Earth is shaped like a ball, the poles get less sunlight. It's also tilted, so they get even less sunlight in winter than in summer. The area near the equator stays warm because it gets plenty of direct sunlight all year round.

ANTARCTIC AIR TEMPERATURE
-10°C (14°F)

Average Antarctic air temperature at sea level by the coast

FROZEN POLES

The temperatures in the Arctic and Antarctic regions can plumet to shockingly low figures. Even so, some animals do manage to survive there—including humans! Many animals have evolved special ways to survive the cold, such as layers of blubber (thick fat) or insulating feathers. Humans have to rely on warm coats and boots instead.

FREEZING POINT OF FRESH WATER
0°C (32°F)

Fresh water is still entirely liquid at 3.9°C (39°F), but any colder and it starts to freeze. As it freezes, the water molecules begin to push away from each other so they take up more space, and the liquid water turns into ice.

-97.8°C (-144°F)

Coldest natural air temperature recorded on Earth This temperature was measured just above the ice near the South Pole in winter, 2018.

TEMPERATURE OF WATER AT ANTARCTIC SEAFLOOR
-1°C (30°F)

Salt water freezes at -2°C (28°F)—a lower temperature than fresh water. This means that the temperature of the water at the bottom of the ocean near Antarctica actually goes just below the freezing point, but the water stays liquid.

MEASURING TEMPERATURE

In order to know exactly how hot or cold something is, we use a thermometer. There are three main temperature scales that are in use today ⟶

FAHRENHEIT (°F)
The Fahrenheit scale was the earliest standard temperature scale to be developed. On this scale, fresh water at sea level freezes at 32 degrees Fahrenheit (32°F) and boils at 212 degrees.

CELSIUS (°C)
The Celsius scale is based on the behavior of water. Zero degrees Celsius (0 °C) is the freezing point of fresh water at sea level, and 100 is the boiling point. It has 100 equal divisions between these two points, so it is also called a centigrade scale.

KELVIN (K)
Today, most scientists use a third scale called the Kelvin scale. It starts at what scientists believe is the lowest possible temperature that could ever happen. This point is called absolute zero.

	°F	°C	K
SURFACE OF THE SUN The Sun is the hottest object in the solar system.	10,000°F	5,538°C	5,810 K
SURFACE OF VENUS With a thick atmosphere that traps heat energy, Venus has the highest surface temperature of all the planets in our solar system.	880°F	471°C	744 K
BOILING POINT OF FRESH WATER AT SEA LEVEL	212°F	100°C	373 K
CURRENT AVERAGE SURFACE TEMPERATURE OF EARTH	59°F	15°C	288 K
FREEZING POINT OF FRESH WATER AT SEA LEVEL	32°F	0°C	273 K
AVERAGE SURFACE TEMPERATURE OF MARS Mars is about 48 billion miles (78 billion km) farther away from the Sun than Earth is, so it's a lot colder.	-80°F	-62°C	210 K
CLOUDS TOPS ON NEPTUNE 2.8 billion miles (4.5 billion km) from the Sun, Neptune's cloud tops are very cold.	-353°F	-214°C	59 K
DEEP SPACE The leftover radiation in the most distant parts of the universe has a temperature just above absolute zero.	-454°F	-270°C	2.7 K

COOL CHEMICALS

Special chemicals can be much colder than temperatures usually found in our everyday world. These temperatures can give them surprising uses.

LIQUID NITROGEN
-196°C to -210°C
(-320°F to -346°F)
This chemical is used in labs and some kitchens to instantly freeze things.

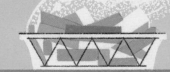

DRY ICE
-78.5°C (-109.3°F)
Instead of being made from water, dry ice is made from carbon dioxide gas that has been cooled under pressure. What's really cool is that when dry ice melts, it does not become a liquid. Instead, it turns back into a frosty, cold gas. This process of turning straight from a solid to a gas is called sublimation.

SUPERCOOLED ELECTROMAGNET
-269°C (-452.2°F)
Engineers have been able to design super-strong electromagnets for use in devices such as MRI scanners, which doctors use to see inside people's bodies. But in order for electromagnets to work properly, they need to be cooled to incredibly cold temperatures. Engineers use liquid helium to keep them this cold.

EARTH IS HOT

There are plenty of places on Earth that are hotter than the average surface temperature of 15°C (59°F), including inside your own body! And when you dig deep, things can warm up even more.

NORMAL BODY TEMPERATURE OF HUMANS
36–37.2°C (97—99°F)
When you get sick, your body fights the attacking germs by raising your temperature a few degrees, giving you a fever.

BODY TEMPERATURE

Most animals are cold-blooded. This means they rely on their environment to keep their bodies at a healthy temperature. But warm-blooded animals, such as birds and mammals, have bodies that control their internal temperatures automatically.

THREE-TOED SLOTH
28°C (82°F)
This slow-moving animal has one of the lowest body temperatures of any mammal.

CHICKEN
42°C (108°F)
Birds have the highest body temperatures of all animals.

WHAT IS HEAT?

The atoms and molecules that make up all the matter in the universe are constantly moving, vibrating back and forth, even in solid objects. Scientists call this movement thermal energy. When thermal energy is added or removed from matter, this is called heat. So, when you heat up a substance its thermal energy increases and the atoms in it vibrate faster.

Temperature is different. It shows how much thermal energy something has, meaning how fast the atoms in it are vibrating. The faster the atoms vibrate in a substance, the higher the temperature. So how cold does a substance have to get to cause the atoms to stop moving completely? That would be absolute zero (-273.15°C, -459.67°F, or 0 K). So far scientists have never found anything this cold, but they are working on it!

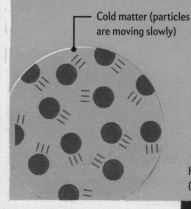

Cold matter (particles are moving slowly)

Hot matter (particles are moving fast)

HOTTEST SURFACE TEMPERATURE ON EARTH
56.7°C (134.1°F)
The "official" record for highest air temperature on Earth was taken in Death Valley, California, on July 10, 1913.

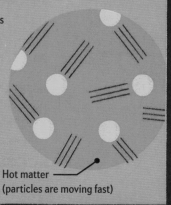

LIGHTNING BOLT
27,760°C (50,000°F)
The temperature of a lighting bolt is hotter than the surface of the Sun!

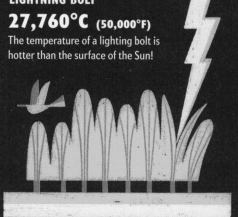

WOOD FIRE
150°C (300°F)
Most wood can start to burn at this temperature, but can reach over 538°C (1,000°F) if conditions are right.

THE INSIDE STORY

While Earth gets most of its heat from the Sun, it also generates some thermal (heat) energy of its own. Scientists have calculated that for every kilometer you go below the surface, the temperature increases by 25°C (77°F). This steady increase is called the geothermal gradient. Because of it, the temperature deep underground can be much higher than on the surface.

HOT PLANET

Earth's surface temperature might be bearable, but below the surface is super-hot rock found in Earth's mantle layer.

HAWAIIAN LAVA
1,170°C (2,140°F)

Some rocks below the surface get so hot they melt, forming magma. This liquid rock can erupt from a volcano as lava. Kilauea volcano on the Big Island of Hawaii has been erupting almost continuously since 1983, bringing up a constant stream of magma from below the Earth's surface.

AVERAGE SURFACE TEMPERATURE
15°C (59°F)

CORE-MANTLE BOUNDARY
6,000°C (10,800°F)

MANTLE
1,000°C (1,832°F)
to 3,700°C (6,692°F)

HEAT IN SPACE

Our Sun is only considered an average star when it comes to temperature, but it's still the hottest object in our solar system. Stars, including the Sun, create light and heat by a process called nuclear fusion. Deep in the center of our star, hydrogen atoms are squeezed together under such high pressures that they form larger helium atoms. This same process powers a hydrogen bomb, and it releases a huge amount of energy, including heat.

QUASAR
10 trillion+°C
(18 trillion+°F)
These super-bright, super-hot objects are found deep in space.

SURFACE OF THE SUN
5,538°C
(10,000°F)

CONVECTION ZONE
2 million°C
(3.6 million°F)

RADIATION ZONE
7 million°C
(12.6 million°F)

SOLAR CORE
15,000,000°C
(27,000,000°F)

MPONENG GOLD MINE
66°C (150°F)
This mine in South Africa reaches 2.5 miles (4 km underground).

EARTH IS WET

Our planet is a wet world. About 71% of its surface is covered by water. For measuring huge volumes like this, scientists use cubic kilometers. One cubic kilometer alone is about 260 billion gallons, and scientists estimate that in total our Earth has about 1.386 billion cubic kilometers of water. That's about the same as 520 trillion Olympic-sized swimming pools! Here's a look at some of the places where water can be found.

SALT WATER AND FRESH WATER

Most of the water that we have on the surface of the Earth is found in the oceans and is called salt water. That's because it contains dissolved minerals that make it taste salty. But most lakes, streams, ponds, and rivers contain fresh water which is the type of water most plants and animals (including humans) that live on land need to survive. Altogether, the total amount of fresh water is about 2.5% of the total water on Earth.

MEASURING VOLUME AND CAPACITY

The amount of liquid that a container can hold is called its capacity. Unlike distance or area, liquids are measured using three-dimensional measurements in units of volume. For example, to find the volume of a container that is 10 cm wide, 10 cm deep, and 10 cm high, you need to multiply the three values together. 10 x 10 x 10 = 1,000, so this gives you a total volume of 1,000 cubic cm, which is the same as one liter.

For smaller volumes, we divide the liter by 1,000 and use milliliters. And for larger volumes, we multiply the liter by 1,000 to get kiloliters. For really massive volumes, such as the amount of water found in an ocean, we use the cubic kilometer which equals 1 trillion liters!

TOTAL VOLUME OF SALT WATER ON EARTH
1.35 billion cubic km
About 97% of Earth's water

FRESH WATER IN GLACIERS AND ICE SHEETS
24 million cubic km
Most of Earth's fresh water is not liquid, but the solid ice of glaciers high in the mountains and ice sheets near the poles. Due to global warming, they are shrinking every day!

TOTAL VOLUME OF FRESH WATER ON EARTH
35 million cubic km
About 3% of Earth's water

GROUNDWATER
10.5 million cubic km
About 0.7% of Earth's water
Hidden deep under the surface is something called groundwater. Over thousands of years, water slowly seeps down through the soil and fills up the tiny spaces and cracks found in the rocks below. People can tap into this water by drilling wells and pumping the water back to the surface.

OTHER FRESH WATER
124,000 cubic km
Most of the remaining fresh water on Earth is found in lakes and rivers, while some is found in the soil, the air, and in living things.

LAKES AND RIVERS

93,000 cubic km

Aside from glaciers and groundwater, most of the rest of Earth's fresh water is found in lakes and rivers. But, altogether, they only make up around 0.4% of the total water on Earth.

AMAZON RIVER

6,300 cubic km

Biggest river by volume of water released
The volume of the Amazon River changes with the seasons. The figure given here is the average volume of water that this enormous river releases into the Atlantic Ocean every year.

LAKE KARIBA

180 cubic km

Largest artificial lake by volume
This human-made lake is located on the Zambezi River between the countries of Zambia and Zimbabwe.

LAKE BAIKAL

23,000 cubic km

Biggest freshwater lake by volume

WATER IN THE SOIL

16,500 cubic km

Before it reaches the rocks deep below the surface, water flows through the soil. Plants use soil water to grow.

WATER IN THE AIR

12,900 cubic km

The constant stream of energy from the Sun causes liquid water on Earth's surface to evaporate. This turns it into a gas called water vapor, but it doesn't stay in the air forever. As the water vapor cools, it condenses and turns back into tiny drops and ice crystals, forming clouds. Eventually, this water falls back to the surface as precipitation in the form of rain or snow, and the cycle can start over again. This continuous movement of water between Earth's surface and the air is called the water cycle.

Water falls back to the surface as precipitation

Water condenses

Water evaporates

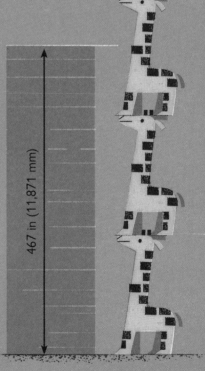

467 in (11,871 mm)

RAINFALL AT CILAOS, REUNION ISLAND, JANUARY 7–8, 1966

72 in
(1,825 mm)

Largest rainfall in a 24-hour period

AVERAGE RAINFALL PER YEAR AT MAWSYNRAM, INDIA

467 in (11,871 mm)

Rainiest spot on Earth • Rainfall varies from year to year, but one place that consistently leads the list of wettest places is Mawsynram, India. It averages almost 40 ft (12 m) of rain a year! That's almost as tall as three giraffes stacked on top of one another.

LIVING WATERS

1,120 cubic km

All living things, from the smallest bacterium to the largest tree, have water in their cells.

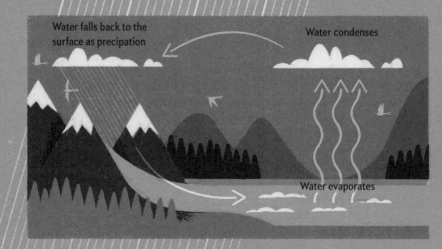

EARTH IS DRY

Even though Earth is believed to have about 1.386 billion cubic kilometer of water on it, scientists estimate that this only makes up about 0.02% of our planet's total mass. Also, all that water isn't very evenly distributed. Our planet is home to some extremely dry places, which we call deserts. And some living things (and some space objects) are practically all water.

WONDERFUL WATER— Why is it so special?

Water is an incredible substance. It is a simple chemical compound that forms when one oxygen atom and two hydrogen atoms bond together. Because of the way the atoms join, a water molecule looks a little like a mouse's head with the oxygen atom making the face and the hydrogen atoms forming the ears.

This special structure gives water molecules an attractive force, allowing them to transport important chemicals around most living things' bodies. It also makes water the "universal solvent." This means that it reacts with most other substances. In fact, given enough time water can wear away even the hardest rock.

DESERT PLANET

Deserts are areas that receive less than 9.8 in (250 mm) of precipitation, such as rain or snow, in a year. They make up about a third of the land surface of Earth.

GREAT BASIN DESERT
189,962 square miles
(492,000 square km)

SONORAN DESERT
120,078 square miles
(311,000 square km)

CHIHUAHUAN DESERT
193,051 square miles
(500,000 square km)

ATACAMA
50,193 square miles
(130,000 square km)
Driest hot desert
Arica, Chile, in the Atacama desert, receives less than 0.03 in (0.76 mm) of rain each year.

SAHARA
3.5 million square miles
(9.1 million square km)
Largest hot desert

NAMIB DESERT
308,882 square miles
(800,000 square km)

KALAHARI DESERT
359,075 square miles
(930,000 square km)

ARABIAN DESERT
1 million square miles
(2.6 million square km)

ANTARCTICA
5.5 million square miles
(14.3 million square km)

Every continent has at least one major desert but one continent is mostly desert: Antarctica. That's right, even though it's covered with a thick layer of ice, much of Antarctica receives less than 2 in (50 mm) of precipitation a year. It has actually taken tens of thousands of years for all the ice to build up on the surface.

The driest spots in the world are found in the dry valleys of Antarctica. Scientists estimate they have received no precipitation in almost 2 million years! As global temperatures increase, desert areas of the world are growing, but the ice in Antarctica is now melting faster than it forms.

FRUITY WATER

Plants need water in order to live. Most land plants have a root system that takes up water from the soil. The water then travels through the plant, carrying nutrients and oxygen up to the leaves. Here the water is used in a process called photosynthesis to make food for the plant. This process also releases oxygen gas into the air. Many plants produce fruit which is often chock-full of water too.

WATERMELON
90% water

GRAPES
80% water

LETTUCE
96% water

GOBI DESERT
501,933 square miles
(1.3 million square km)

GREAT VICTORIA DESERT
250,966 square miles
(650,000 square km)

WATER IN THE SOLAR SYSTEM

Earth isn't the only object in the solar system that has water on it. Scientists have discovered large amounts of water throughout the solar system.

Some of the most water-rich objects are comets, which are often referred to as "dirty snowballs." These icy chunks from far out in the solar system can be as much as 80% water by mass, far more than Earth's 0.02%. Some scientists believe that some of the water found on Earth today was actually delivered by comets early in our history.

EUROPA
3 billion cubic km of water
20% of total volume • Moon of Jupiter
Jupiter's moon Europa is covered with a thick layer of ice. Astronomers think that underneath this icy crust might be a large ocean of water. It could be as much as 62 miles (100 km) deep and contain more than twice the volume of all the water on Earth.

TITAN
18 billion cubic km of water
25% of total volume • Moon of Saturn
Titan is larger than the planet Mercury. Like Europa, it is believed to have a frozen layer of ice on the surface covering an enormous liquid ocean below.

An average adult has about 72 pints (34 liters) of water in their body. Most of this is found inside cells. You have trillions of them in your body, and each one has water in it. When you add it all up, the total volume of water in the cells alone can be as much as 59 pints (28 liters).

WATER IN YOUR BODY

You're all wet! That's not an insult, it's just scientific fact. The human body is full of water. Blood is mostly water. You also have water in your digestive tract, and you excrete a lot of water every time you pee. To stay healthy, doctors recommend that you should drink about 4.2 pints (two liters) of water per day. So how much water does your body contain? That depends on your age.

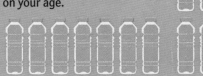

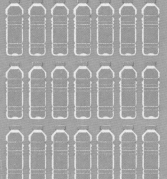

AVERAGE ADULT
55–60% water

AVERAGE CHILD
65% water

AVERAGE NEWBORN
75% water

EARTH IS FAST

At this very second you, along with everyone else on Earth, are flying through space at approximately 66,480 miles per hour (107,000 km/h). That's based on Earth orbiting the Sun at an average speed of 18.6 miles per second (30 km/s). Let's see how this compares to the speed of some other familiar objects.

THINGS IN SPACE

Earth has two motions. First, it is orbiting, or revolving, around the Sun. We call the speed Earth's orbital speed.

But Earth is also spinning in place like a giant top. The spinning motion is called rotation, and it's why we have day and night. This speed is called rotational speed. Because Earth is shaped like a ball, the rotational speed is different depending on where you are standing on the planet. At either pole your rotational speed would be almost nothing because you would basically be spinning in place. At the equator, though, you would be whipping along at about 1,038 mph (1,670 km/h).

ORBITAL SPEED OF THE EARTH
66,480 mph
(107,000 km/h)

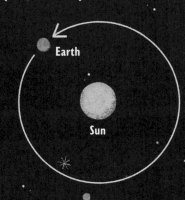

Earth

Sun

ROTATIONAL SPEED OF THE EARTH
1,038 mph
(1,670 km/h)

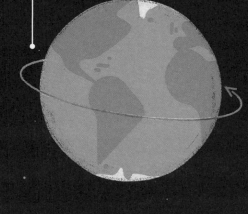

ROTATIONAL SPEED OF THE MOON
9.9 mph
(16 km/h)
The Moon, our closest neighbor in space, orbits the Earth. Like the Earth, the Moon is also rotating on its axis, but at a much slower speed—9.9 mph (16 km/h) at its equator—about as fast as you ride your bike. It completes one spin every 27.32 days.

ORBITAL SPEED OF INTERNATIONAL SPACE STATION
17,398 mph
(28,000 km/h)
The ISS is suspended in orbit above the Earth. Rockets blast off regularly from Earth to bring supplies and shuttle crew back and forth. On board scientists run experiments and study life in space.

ORBITAL SPEED OF THE MOON
2,287 mph
(3,681 km/h)

ORBITAL SPEED OF CERES
39,991 mph
(64,360 km/h)
Ceres is a dwarf planet located in the asteroid belt between Mars and Jupiter.

Ceres

Sun

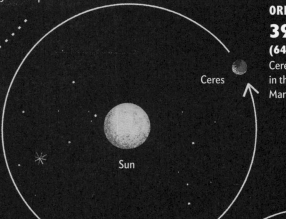

MEASURING SPEED

Speed is the measurement that shows how fast something is moving. To figure out the speed of an object, you need to know the distance the object travels and the amount of time it takes to get there. You then divide the distance by the time taken. For example, if a car travels 50 miles in one hour, then the speed is 50 miles per hour (usually written 50 mph).

Depending on the speed of the object, you can use different units. High speeds, like the speed of the Earth moving around the Sun, are measured in miles or km per second (miles/s or km/s). Something slow, like the speed of a snail or turtle, might be measured in inches or meters per hour (in/h or m/h).

ORBITAL SPEED OF PLUTO
10,563 mph
(17,000 km/h)
The orbit of Pluto is slightly oval and off-center.

Pluto

Sun

TOP SPEEDS

From the super fast to the super slow, Earth is full of animals and vehicles going places at different speeds.

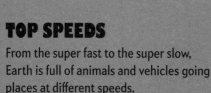

0 KM/H

SNAIL
0.03 mph
(0.05 km/h)

TORTOISE
0.62 mph
(1 km/h)

HUMAN
28 mph (45 km/h)
Top speed (Usain Bolt) • Humans can sprint fast over short distances but tend to tire quickly, so don't even think about trying to outrun a lion.

LION
50 mph (80 km/h)

WILDEBEEST
50 mph
(80 km/h)

100 KM/H

PASSENGER JET
497 mph
(800 km/h)
Cruising speed

SPIRIT OF AUSTRALIA
318 mph
(511 km/h)
Fastest marine vehicle • From the first canoes to atomic-powered submarines, humans have used a wide range of vehicles to move through water. The current record for fastest boat was set in 1978 by the *Spirit of Australia*.

PEREGRINE FALCON
236 mph (380 km/h)
Fastest animal (speed when diving)

FORMULA 1 CAR
233 mph
(375 km/h)
Top speed

MARLIN
80 mph (129 km/h)
Fastest marine animal • The bodies of some fish, such as the sailfish, swordfish, and marlin, are built for speed.

CHEETAH
70 mph
(113 km/h)
Fastest land animal

1,000 KM/H

10,000 KM/H

THRUST SSC
763 mph
(1,228 km/h)
Fastest land vehicle • This super-fast car is powered by two jet engines.

SR-71 BLACKBIRD
2,193 mph (3,529 km/h)
Super-fast military jet

X-15 ROCKET PLANE
4,520 mph (7,274 km/h)
Fastest manned airplane

**SPEED OF SOUND
AT SEA LEVEL AT 20°C (68°F)**
768 mph
(1,235 km/h / 343 m/s)

SPEED OF SOUND

Sound is created when something vibrates, and these vibrations move out as waves through different types of matter. Air temperature, elevation, and humidity can affect the speed of sound. Because water molecules are packed closer together, sound travels almost four times faster in pure water than in air.

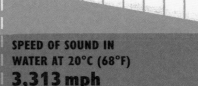

**SPEED OF SOUND IN
WATER AT 20°C (68°F)**
3,313 mph
(5,332 km/h / 1,481 m/s)

EARTH IS SLOW

Even though our planet is speeding around the Sun at over 66,480 miles per hour (107,000 km/h), there are plenty of things that make Earth look slow. Here are some of the fastest things in our universe.

SPEEDING THROUGH THE SOLAR SYSTEM

There is a lot of motion in the solar system. Here are some of the fastest objects.

ORBITAL SPEED OF EARTH
66,480 mph
(107,000 km/h)
Earth takes 365.25 days to complete one orbit around the Sun—that's a year to you and me!

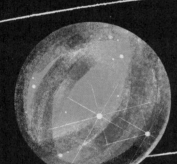

ORBITAL SPEED OF MERCURY
106,031 mph
(171,640 km/h)
Mercury is the closest planet to the Sun. It takes only 88 days to complete one orbit.

ORBITAL SPEED OF VENUS
78,293 mph
(126,000 km/h)
Venus takes 225 days to complete one orbit around the Sun.

Speed of Light

The speed of sound may seem very quick at about 768 mph (1,235 km/h) at sea level at 20°C, but it's pretty slow compared to the speed of light. In fact, light is the fastest thing in the universe. The exact speed of light in a vacuum is 299,792,458 m/s or a little under 186,282 miles per second (299,792 km/s). At this speed it takes light about 8 minutes and 19 seconds to reach Earth from the Sun.

FAST BLASTS FROM THE SUN

Our Sun is constantly sending out energy and particles, which travel at incredibly fast speeds. Energy from the Sun is essential to life on Earth, but powerful blasts of it can also be dangerous.

CORONAL MASS EJECTIONS
6.7 million mph
(10.8 million km/h)
Every so often the Sun releases a big blast of charged particles called a coronal mass ejection (CME). When these happen, the solar wind can more than double in speed.

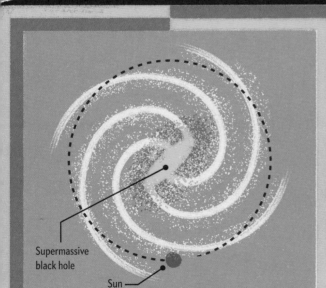

Supermassive black hole

Sun

ORBITAL SPEED OF THE SUN AROUND THE MILKY WAY
507,785 mph (817,200 km/h)
Planets orbit the Sun, and moons orbit planets. But what about the Sun, does it orbit anything? Along with the rest of the stars in the Milky Way, our Sun is orbiting around a supermassive black hole at the galaxy's center. Because the galaxy is so large, it takes roughly 230 million years to complete one orbit.

SOLAR WIND
894,775 mph
(1.44 million km/h)
In addition to the light that we see, the Sun also sends out a steady stream of charged particles into space called the solar wind. When these particles hit Earth's magnetic field, they create the Northern and Southern lights.

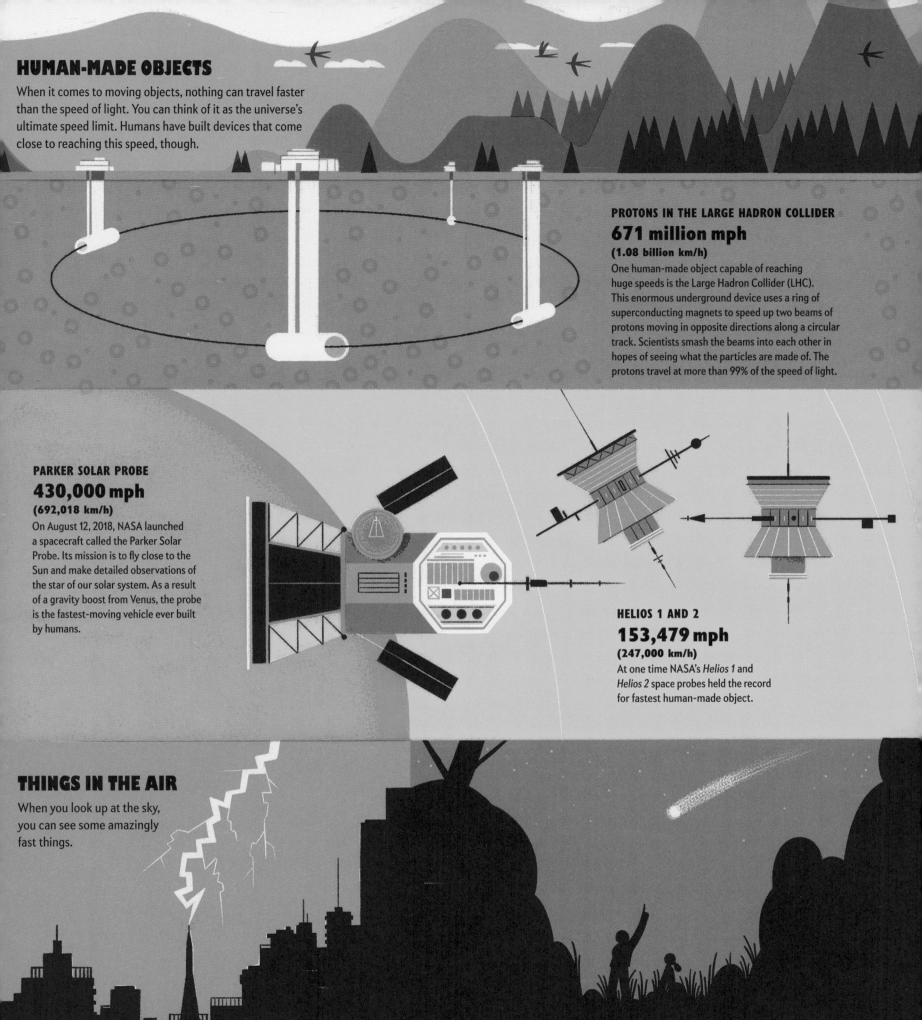

HUMAN-MADE OBJECTS

When it comes to moving objects, nothing can travel faster than the speed of light. You can think of it as the universe's ultimate speed limit. Humans have built devices that come close to reaching this speed, though.

PROTONS IN THE LARGE HADRON COLLIDER
671 million mph
(1.08 billion km/h)

One human-made object capable of reaching huge speeds is the Large Hadron Collider (LHC). This enormous underground device uses a ring of superconducting magnets to speed up two beams of protons moving in opposite directions along a circular track. Scientists smash the beams into each other in hopes of seeing what the particles are made of. The protons travel at more than 99% of the speed of light.

PARKER SOLAR PROBE
430,000 mph
(692,018 km/h)

On August 12, 2018, NASA launched a spacecraft called the Parker Solar Probe. Its mission is to fly close to the Sun and make detailed observations of the star of our solar system. As a result of a gravity boost from Venus, the probe is the fastest-moving vehicle ever built by humans.

HELIOS 1 AND 2
153,479 mph
(247,000 km/h)

At one time NASA's *Helios 1* and *Helios 2* space probes held the record for fastest human-made object.

THINGS IN THE AIR

When you look up at the sky, you can see some amazingly fast things.

LIGHTNING STRIKE
270,000 mph
(434,523 km/h)

One thing up in the air that is sure to catch your eye is a bolt of lightning, which is caused by static electricity.

METEOR
29,826 mph
(48,000 km/h)

Have your ever seen a "shooting star" whizzing through the night sky? These streaks of light are actually chunks of rocks from space that burn up as they move through the atmosphere.

EARTH IS ROUND

Almost nothing in the universe is perfectly round, but our planet comes very close. Earth still has some imperfections, though. Here's how it compares to some other round objects that can be found both on Earth and in outer space.

SPHERES AND SPHEROIDS

The Earth might look like a perfectly round ball but when scientists were able to measure it, they discovered that it is not the same size in all directions. Because of its rotation, Earth is flattened a bit at the poles and bulges out at the equator. Earth's diameter at the equator is 7,926 miles (12,756 km). But if you measure the diameter through the poles instead, it is only 7,900 miles (12,714 km).

This small difference means that the Earth is not a perfect sphere. Instead, it's a slightly flattened shape that scientists call an oblate spheroid—although it's still pretty round!

SOAP BUBBLE

One example of a perfect sphere here on Earth is a soap bubble. When you blow soap bubbles, they often start off with an irregular shape. But once they are floating in the air, they usually pull themselves into perfect spheres. The reason for this is a force called surface tension, which is present between the water molecules in the soap. The water molecules tug on each other equally in all directions. This causes them to pull the bubble into a perfect sphere.

WATER DROPS IN SPACE

The surface tension of water causes drops to form perfect spheres when astronauts allow them to "free fall" inside the International Space Station.

KEPLER 11145123

Rarely do planets and stars form perfect spheres, but astronomers have found one star that comes really close. It's a star about 5,000 light-years from Earth and is called Kepler 11145123. It is the most spherical object in space that astronomers have discovered so far.

NOT QUITE SPHERES

Like the Earth, many other objects in nature can appear spherical but are actually other shapes.

RAINDROPS

When water drops are floating in clouds, they are tiny and are almost spherical in shape. As they grow, they become heavier and start to fall to Earth as rain. This downward motion also causes them to flatten out a bit. This makes the raindrop's shape more like a dome than the classic "teardrop" shape that most people think of.

LUMPY AND BUMPY IN SPACE

Larger objects in space usually take the form of spheroids, but a few do have some very unusual shapes.

VESTA

Vesta is the second-largest known asteroid with a diameter of about 330 miles (530 km). Images taken by NASA's *Dawn* spacecraft show it to be an irregularly shaped oblate spheroid. Its surface is dotted with lots of craters.

DEIMOS AND PHOBOS

Mars has two small moons orbiting it named Deimos and Phobos. They are both shaped a little like potatoes.

ULTIMA THULE

This small icy world orbits the Sun about 4 billion miles (6.5 billion km) from Earth. It has a flat shape like a long pancake. The shape is so unusual that scientists are puzzled how Ultimate Thule formed.

YOUR EYE

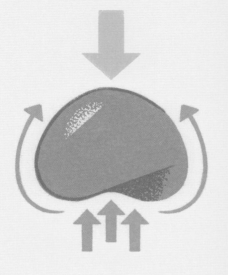

The human eyeball is not a perfect sphere. It is slightly flatter at the front and tapers toward the back. Even tiny changes in the shape of the eye can create different vision problems.

REPTILE EGGS

Reptile eggs come in different shapes and sizes, and all have rounded sides. Some turtle eggs are almost perfect spheres, while crocodile eggs are oval.

Owl egg   Ostrich egg   Emu egg   Sandpiper egg   Snake egg   Crocodile egg   Turtle egg

BIRD EGGS

Bird eggs come in different sizes and all have rounded sides. They range from near spherical for owls to cone shaped for sandpipers.

SPORTS BALLS

Both billiard and bowling balls need to be perfect spheres to make them roll well. But some of the other sports balls have unusual shapes, especially those that are kicked!

RUGBY BALL

A rugby ball is a prolate spheroid. This means that it is a three-dimensional, stretched-out oval with two rounded ends. While modern rugby balls are made of leather, the original shape is said to have come from people using an inflated pig's bladder as a ball.

FOOTBALL

Like rugby balls, footballs are also prolate spheroids, except they have pointed ends and heavy laces which makes them easier to throw.

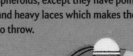

SOCCER BALL

Traditional soccer balls have 32 panels of six-sided hexagons and five-sided pentagons covering the surface. The technical name for this type of mostly round shape is a truncated icosahedron.

EARTH IS JAGGED

From space, Earth looks like a smooth round ball. But when you get down to the surface, you can see just how rough and jagged our planet is. Here's a look at some of the famous high points and low spots found around our world.

RUPPELL'S GRIFFON VULTURE
around 36,900 ft
(11,250 m)
Highest flying bird

THINGS UP HIGH

Earth is loaded with mountains that stick up from the surface. Some, like Mt. Kilimanjaro in Tanzania, sit by themselves while others, like the Matterhorn in Switzerland, are parts of large mountain chains.

Measurements on this page reflect height above or below sea level.

PASSENGER JET
around 32,800 ft
(10,000 m)
Cruising altitude

MT. EVEREST
29,032 ft
(8,849 m)
Mt. Everest is the highest mountain in the world. It is part of the Himalayan mountain range in Asia, which includes all but one of the ten tallest mountains on Earth.

MAUNA KEA
13,795 ft
(4,205 m)
While Mt. Everest is the highest mountain, the Mauna Kea volcano in Hawaii is the tallest mountain when measured from its base to its top even though the summit is only 4,025 m above sea level.

While the base of Mt. Everest is at sea level, the base of Mauna Kea actually sits underwater, about 6,000 m below sea level. With a total height of 10,210 m it is roughly 1,361 m taller than Mt. Everest.

CHIMBORAZO
20,564 ft
(6,310 m)
Mt. Everest may be the highest place above sea level, but the top of the Chimborazo volcano in Ecuador is furthest from Earth's actual center. The reason for this difference is because Chimborazo sits at a point on the planet's surface that is bulging out due to Earth's daily rotation.

32,800 FT (10,000 M)

24,600 FT (7,500 M)

16,400 FT (5,000 M)

8,200 FT (2,500 M)

0 FT (SEA LEVEL

MEASURING ELEVATIONS

When scientists measure how high or low a place is, they need to compare it to a reference point on the planet's surface that is not going to change very quickly. This "zero point" is called a datum. The datum that is most often used to measure elevations on Earth is mean sea level. Mean is another word for "average," and mean sea level was originally defined as the height of the ocean right between high and low tide. At first scientists used the real height of the sea.

However, because sea level is always changing there is a problem with using it as a datum. To solve the problem, a group of scientists called geodesists collected lots of data and agreed on a figure for a worldwide sea level that never changes. Today GPS systems that measure elevations on Earth use this figure to work correctly.

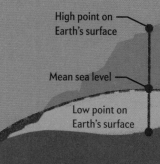

High point on Earth's surface

Mean sea level

Low point on Earth's surface

HERBERT NITSCH
830 ft below sea level
(253 m)
Deepest free dive

RMS *TITANIC*
12,500 ft below sea level
(3,800 m)
Shipwreck

-8,200 FT (-2,500 M)

STEEP DROPS

Mountains can be very high, and valleys can be very low, but when it comes to seeing just how jagged the surface of the Earth is, there is nothing like the sharp drop of a cliff. Unlike the side of most mountains, which have a slope, cliffs are sheer drops that go straight up and down.

WHITE CLIFFS OF DOVER
About 328 ft (100 m)
Located in the UK, these are some of the most famous sea cliffs in the world.

EL CAPITAN
7,569 ft (2,307 m)
One of the most spectacular cliffs in the world, El Capitan features a 3,600 ft (1,100 m) vertical drop and is located in Yosemite National Park in California. This giant mass of granite rock is a favorite of rock climbers.

ANGEL FALLS
3,212 ft (979 m)
Some cliffs have water flowing over them, producing spectacular waterfalls. Angel Falls in Venezuela has the highest total drop of any waterfall in the world.

THINGS DOWN LOW

Rivers and glaciers can carve deep canyons and trenches through the Earth's surface. And there are valleys on the ocean floor, too. Some of the valleys are incredibly deep. The deepest valleys, called ocean trenches, can be found at the edge of continental plates in all the major oceans.

GRAND CANYON
5,249 ft average depth below land surface (1,600 m)
This 227-mile (446-km)-long gorge in the western United States has been carved into the Earth by the Colorado River.

BENTLEY SUBGLACIAL TRENCH
8,382 ft below sea level (2,555 m)
This is the lowest point on Earth not covered by an ocean. Reaching this point is impossible, though, because it is under several thousand meters of Antarctic ice.

CHALLENGER DEEP
36,200 ft below sea level (11,034 m)
The lowest point on Earth's surface is called the Challenger Deep. It can be found in one of the low points in the Earth's crust called the Mariana Trench, an ocean trench in the Pacific Ocean near the Philippines.

BIG BUILDINGS

Natural landforms aren't the only thing that give our planet a jagged surface. During the last 5,000 years or so, humans have done a good job of creating pretty impressive structures. Some of these can reach incredible heights.

BURJ KHALIFA
2,716 ft tall (828 m)
As of 2021, this building in Dubai, UAE, is the tallest building in the world. Records are made to be broken, and construction of even taller structures is already in the works.

GREAT PYRAMID
481 ft tall (146 m)
Even by today's standards, the Great Pyramid in Egypt is a massive structure, and for almost 3,800 years it was the tallest building in the world.

EARTH IS HEAVY

Earth is chock-full of matter, including rocks, water, gases such as air, and lots of living things. All of this stuff makes our planet a real heavyweight, with an estimated mass of about 6.6 sextillion tons (6 septillion kg)—a sextillion is a 1 followed by 21 zeros!

THINGS IN SPACE

Our solar system is full of objects lighter than Earth, including moons, asteroids, and dwarf planets.

EARTH
6.6 sextillion tons
(6 septillion kg)

MARS
700 quintillion tons
(642 sextillion kg)

Rocky planet • Earth has a mass that is about 9.3 times greater than that of Mars.

GANYMEDE
163 quintillion tons
(148 sextillion kg)

Moon of Jupiter • The largest moon in the solar system, Ganymede's diameter is bigger than the planet Mercury's, and almost half the size of Earth's. But Ganymede is made mostly out of frozen gases and water, while Earth is made mostly out of rock, which is much heavier. So it would take about 40 Ganymedes to equal Earth's mass.

OUR MOON
8.1 quintillion tons
(73.5 sextillion kg)

The current mass of our Moon is estimated to be about 8,100,000,000,000,000,000 (that's 8.1 quintillion) tons (73.5 sextillion kg). This means that it would take the mass of 81 moons to equal the mass of our planet.

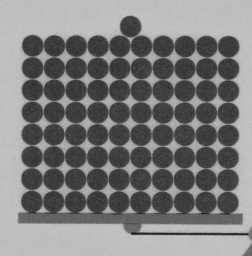

MEGA MACHINES

Enormous trains, trucks, and planes are used every day to move objects and people around the world. Some of these are among the heaviest objects ever built by humans.

LEXUS LX
5,998 lb
(2,721 kg)
Heavy modern car

UNION PACIFIC "CENTENNIAL"
551,155 lb
(250,000 kg)
Train locomotive

BELAZ 75710
793,664 lb
(360,000 kg)
Dump truck

MASS OR WEIGHT?

People often confuse the terms mass and weight. Even though they are related, they do not mean the same thing. Mass is a measure of how much matter or "stuff" an object contains. It's measured in units such as pounds (lb) or kilograms (kg). Mass tells you how hard it is to move something—the more mass it has, the more difficult it is to move.

But weight is different—it's a measure of how much the force of gravity acts on an object. It's measured in pounds of force (lbf). On Earth's surface, mass and weight behave in the same way because the force of gravity is mostly the same all over the planet. But travel to the Moon, where the force of gravity is around 1/6th of the amount on Earth, and you'll notice the difference. Let's say you have a mass of 110 lb (50 kg). On Earth you would weigh 110 lbf. If you traveled to the Moon your mass would still be the same—110 lb (50 kg)—but your weight would now be just 18 lbf.

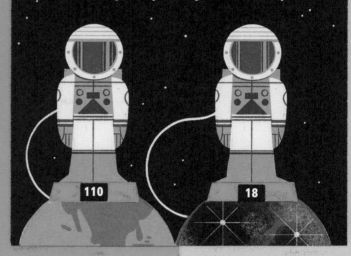

AIRBUS A380 AIRPLANE
123,458 lb
(560,000 kg)

Passenger jet plane • When we think of things flying through the air, we usually picture objects that have very little mass. These could be balloons, feathers, or the white puffy seeds of dandelions. But enormous passenger jet planes can fly too! The Airbus A380 is the current record holder for largest passenger airplane. It can seat over 800 people and carry more than 3,000 pieces of baggage.

RMS *TITANIC*
92,500,000 lb
(42,000,000 kg)

Passenger liner • One of the most famous ships ever built, the RMS *Titanic* and was supposed to be unsinkable, but it did just that after it hit an iceberg in 1912. At the time, it was the biggest ocean liner ever built.

EARTH IS LIGHT

While Earth has a great deal of mass, the rocks that make up its crust are not very heavy compared to many other objects that have the same size. Here's how the density of a typical Earth rock stacks up against some other objects.

INSIDE THE EARTH

The Earth is made up of layers of different types of rocks and minerals, from the outer crust that humans live on, through the mantle and liquid outer core, to its solid inner core.

CRUST

3 g per cm³
(grams per cubic centimeter)

Outer layer of the Earth • Some of the densest rocks found in the Earth's outer layer, or crust, are made from igneous rocks. These rocks, such as basalt and peridotite, contain heavy elements such as iron and magnesium. They form when hot liquid rock called magma cools and turns solid. Even with these rocks, the crust isn't as dense as Earth's interior.

MANTLE

4.4 g per cm³

Middle layer of the Earth • Earth's mantle is the layer below the crust. Here the rocks are under such high pressure that they are denser than the crust and can actually flow like toothpaste.

CORE

13 g per cm³

Central part of the Earth • Earth's core is made of two parts. First, there is a liquid outer core. Within that is an inner core that is thought to be a very dense and solid mass of iron and nickel.

MEASURING DENSITY

Measuring the mass of an object tells you the amount of stuff, known as matter, it has in it, but to get an idea of how tightly packed together the matter is inside an object, we need to measure a property called density. Density is the relationship between the mass of an object and the amount of space it takes up, or volume, measured in grams per cubic centimeter (g per cm³).

To calculate the density of an object you divide its total mass by its total volume. The average density of rocks on Earth's continents is about 3 g/cm³. But, if you take the entire mass of the Earth and divide by its volume, the average density of our planet is higher, about 5.5 g/cm³. This difference shows that most of the Earth is more dense than the rocks we see on the surface.

A bowling ball is heavier than a beach ball of the same size because it is more dense.

THINGS IN SPACE

The densest objects in the universe are found in outer space.

NEUTRON STAR

500 trillion g per cm³

Astronomers believe that a neutron star is the core of a supermassive star after it has gone through a supernova explosion. These incredibly compact objects are the densest-known objects in the universe.

THE SUN'S CORE

150 g per cm³

Our Sun is made of super-hot hydrogen and helium gas. On Earth, these gases have extremely low densities. That's why balloons filled with them float in the air. But when you put these gases under extremely high pressure, the density skyrockets. While, overall, the Sun's density is only about 1.4 g/cm³, scientists estimate that the density of its core is as high as 150 g/cm³.

HEAVY METALS

When it comes to high densities, metals generally are the leaders of the pack. Precious metals are treasured by people across the globe just for how they look or how rare they are, but most metals can have other uses too.

ALUMINUM
2.7 g per cm³

This shiny metal isn't considered a heavy metal because it has a low density. This makes it useful for objects that need to be light and strong, such as jet planes. Even though it's a metal, it's only about 3 times as dense as an average human body.

COPPER
8.9 g per cm³

This metal is an excellent conductor of heat and electricity and is used in wiring and cookware.

IRON
7.9 g per cm³

This strong metal is attracted to magnets and is used in construction.

SILVER
10.5 g per cm³

This shiny metal is used for decorative items and jewelry.

LEAD
11.3 g per cm³

This heavy metal is frequently used to make batteries for cars and other equipment.

MERCURY
13.6 g per cm³

Unlike most metals, mercury is a liquid at typical surface temperatures on Earth. Until about 10 years ago, this silvery metal was used in thermometers.

GOLD
19.3 g per cm³

People have cherished gold for thousands of years. Humans have used it to make jewelry and decorative items. Because it's also an excellent conductor of electricity, we use it in modern electronic equipment such as cell phones, too. Gold is one of the denser metals found on Earth.

PLATINUM
21.5 g per cm³

This metal is used in everything from jewelry to the spark plugs in car engines.

EARTH CHANGES QUICKLY

Our planet is always changing. In many cases these changes happen very quickly. Some happen over the course of months or years, but others can take only a matter of hours.

IN THE AIR

The atmosphere is a complex mixture of gases. It is mostly made of the elements nitrogen and oxygen. Earth's atmosphere also contains smaller amounts of more than a dozen other gases, including water vapor.

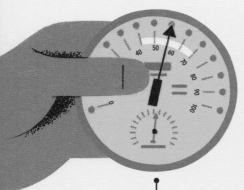

HUMIDITY

The amount of water vapor in the air, called humidity, is constantly changing. Scientists use a device called a hygrometer to measure it. The closer the humidity gets to 100% the more chance of precipitation happening.

AIR PRESSURE

The force of the air pushing against Earth's surface is called air pressure. It is always changing, and scientists measure it with a device called a barometer.

WIND

Winds change direction and speed constantly, but they always blow from areas of high air pressure to areas of low air pressure. Wind speed is measured using a device called an anemometer.

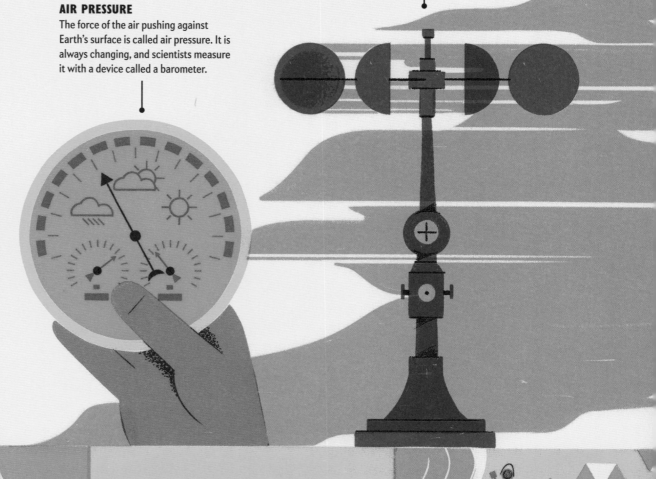

ON THE SURFACE

It might seem that Earth's continents and oceans mostly stay the same, but geological and tidal forces can quickly reshape entire landmasses.

EARTHQUAKES

Earthquakes happen when two sections of Earth's crust suddenly slide past each other. They can occur with little or no warning, destroying buildings, bridges, and roads, and creating massive landslides. Scientists measure the strength of an earthquake using a device called a seismograph.

TIDES

Tides happen twice a day when the level of the ocean moves up and down. You can see this on a beach from how the water's edge moves back and forth throughout the day. The tides are caused by tiny shifts in the Moon's and Sun's gravitational pull on the Earth's surface.

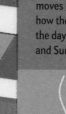

VOLCANOES

Volcanoes are openings in Earth's crust where melted rock called magma moves up from below and then flows onto the surface as lava and ash, creating new land. Scientists estimate that there are about 1,500 potentially active volcanoes on Earth right now. About 500 have erupted in historical times. When massive volcanoes like Mount Pinatubo in the Philippines erupt, they bring about sudden changes to both the land surface and the atmosphere.

THINGS IN THE SKY

The position and movement of objects in space can have a surprising effect on Earth.

SUNRISE AND SUNSET

Sunrise and sunset each day are caused by Earth spinning on its axis. When your part of Earth faces the Sun it is day. When your part faces away from the Sun, it is night.

THE SEASONS

If you are a careful observer and you don't live near the equator, you can see that the Sun's path across the sky changes just a bit each day. This happens because Earth is tilted on its axis. As we move around in our orbit, the direct light from the Sun is focused on a slightly different place on Earth each day. This steady change creates the seasons, and it's also why the number of minutes of daylight changes each day.

MOON PHASES

Throughout each month, the Moon appears to change shape from a thin crescent to a full circle and back again. This is the lunar phase cycle, and it takes 29.5 days to complete. It happens because we see different amounts of the lit up side of the Moon as it orbits the Earth.

WANDERING PLANETS

When you look at the night sky, you will see lots of bright dots. Most of these are stars, but some of the really bright ones are planets. Over time the stars will move across the night sky in a particular pattern. While their location in the sky changes, their pattern doesn't. But the planets don't follow the same pattern as the stars, they can speed up, slow down, and even appear to move backwards.

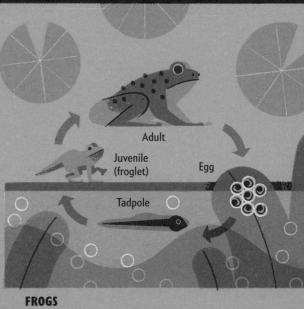

LIVING THINGS CHANGE

All animals, including humans, go through a series of changes throughout their lifetimes, called a life cycle.

HUMAN GROWTH

When we are first born, we are helpless babies that require lots of care. By the time we are about 2 years old, we can walk and talk. Not long after, we change from toddlers into rapidly growing children. When we become teenagers, we reach adolescence and go through more changes until we reach adulthood.

BUTTERFLIES

Butterflies and all other insects also go through big changes over the course of their lives. This process is called metamorphosis. After they hatch from eggs, the babies, called larva, take the form of a caterpillar. Next, during the pupa stage, the caterpillar creates a covering around itself called a chrysalis. Eventually it emerges from its chrysalis as an adult butterfly.

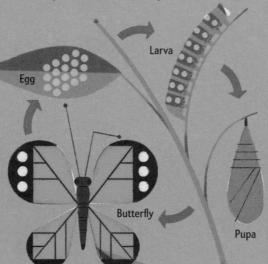

Egg

Larva

Butterfly

Pupa

FROGS

Frogs, like butterflies, go through a type of metamorphosis. After hatching from eggs in water, they become tadpoles, which look like little fish. As they mature, they grow legs, lose their tails, and change into adult frogs.

Adult

Juvenile (froglet)

Egg

Tadpole

EARTH CHANGES SLOWLY

Some Earth changes take place so slowly that you can't even see them happen during a person's lifetime. Here's a look at some of the slow-motion changes happening to our planet even if you don't notice them.

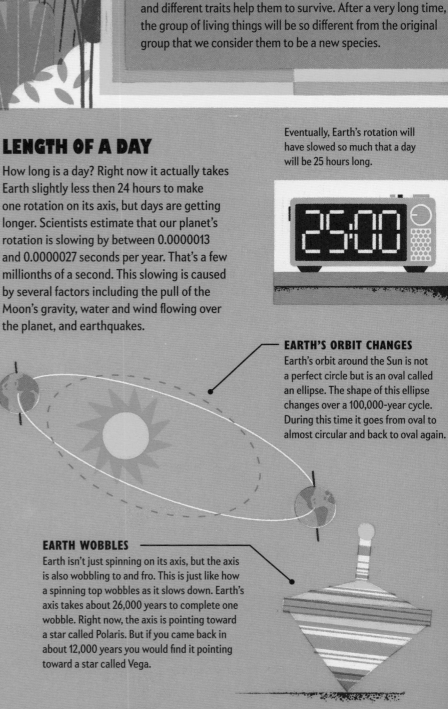

LIVING THINGS CHANGE

The process of natural selection works very slowly. It usually takes thousands, if not millions, of years for new species to evolve. Today, mammals are an incredibly diverse group of animals, but they all developed from a single group.

MONOTREME MAMMALS

Scientists believe that the first mammals laid eggs just like reptiles and amphibians. Only two egg-laying mammals are still around today: the platypus and the echidna. These both belong to a group called monotremes and live in Australia.

PLACENTAL MAMMALS

Most modern mammals belong to a group called placentals. In this group, which includes humans, the baby fully develops inside the mother. Then, after she gives birth, she feeds the baby with milk and cares for it.

MARSUPIAL MAMMALS

Marsupials, such as kangaroos, are a small group of mammals from an older original group. Among marsupials, the baby does not fully develop until after it is born. Its development takes place in the mother's special pouch.

NATURAL SELECTION AND EVOLUTION

In 1859, naturalist Charles Darwin published a groundbreaking book now known as *Origin of Species*. In it, he outlined his theory of evolution and explained how different life forms change over time due to a process called natural selection.

Here's how it works. Within a group of living things, some individuals have certain abilities called traits that allows them to survive better than others. As the others die off, the survivors pass their more useful traits onto their offspring. Over time, each new generation has slightly different traits from the one before them because their environment changes and different traits help them to survive. After a very long time, the group of living things will be so different from the original group that we consider them to be a new species.

LENGTH OF A DAY

How long is a day? Right now it actually takes Earth slightly less then 24 hours to make one rotation on its axis, but days are getting longer. Scientists estimate that our planet's rotation is slowing by between 0.0000013 and 0.0000027 seconds per year. That's a few millionths of a second. This slowing is caused by several factors including the pull of the Moon's gravity, water and wind flowing over the planet, and earthquakes.

Eventually, Earth's rotation will have slowed so much that a day will be 25 hours long.

EARTH'S ORBIT CHANGES

Earth's orbit around the Sun is not a perfect circle but is an oval called an ellipse. The shape of this ellipse changes over a 100,000-year cycle. During this time it goes from oval to almost circular and back to oval again.

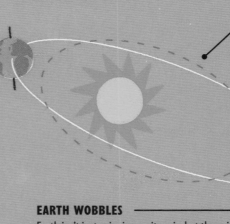

EARTH WOBBLES

Earth isn't just spinning on its axis, but the axis is also wobbling to and fro. This is just like how a spinning top wobbles as it slows down. Earth's axis takes about 26,000 years to complete one wobble. Right now, the axis is pointing toward a star called Polaris. But if you came back in about 12,000 years you would find it pointing toward a star called Vega.

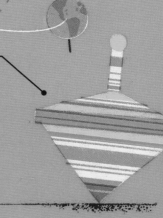

EARTH'S SURFACE

If you look at a map of Earth, it almost looks like some of the continents could be fit together like pieces from a giant jigsaw puzzle. Over the last 100 years, scientists also noticed this and using data from earthquakes and volcanoes developed an idea call plate tectonics. This theory says that Earth's crust is divided into about two dozen giant chunks called tectonic plates. Each plate is slowly moving around the surface. We don't normally feel this motion because even the fastest plates only move about 4 in (10 cm) per year.

North American plate

Eurasian plate

Pacific plate

Arabian plate

Caribbean plate

Indian plate

Philippine plate

African plate

Nazca plate

South American plate

Australian plate

Antarctic plate

GROWTH OF THE HIMALAYAS
The Himalayas are the highest mountains in the world. They started forming about 50 million years ago when the tectonic plate below India crashed into the Eurasian plate. They are still getting taller every year by about 0.4 in (1 cm).

Indian plate

Eurasian plate

200 million years ago

100 million years ago

Present day

EROSION—ULURU
Water and wind are not solids like rock, but over a long time they can wear it away in a process called erosion. Uluru—also known as Ayers Rock—in Australia sticks up today because about 300 million years of wind erosion has worn away the softer rock that surrounded it.

IN THE AIR

Earth's atmosphere is composed of gases, including the oxygen we need to breathe. However, the gases in the atmosphere have changed a great deal over Earth's lifetime.

CLIMATE
When scientists talk about climate, they are talking about the temperature and amount of precipitation that an area gets over a long period of time. Earth's climate is always changing, but the changes usually happen quite slowly over the course of thousands of years.

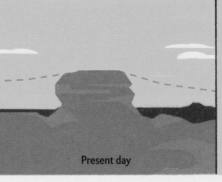

CHANGES IN THE ATMOSPHERE
Soon after the planet formed, volcanoes released large amounts of carbon dioxide, water vapor, and several other gases. Unlike today, there was very little oxygen in the atmosphere at this time. Beginning around 3 billion years ago, photosynthetic organisms started using carbon dioxide in the air to make food and replaced it with oxygen. Over time the atmosphere slowly came to resemble today's: about 78% nitrogen, 21% oxygen, and only 0.03% carbon dioxide.

But over the past 300 years, the amount of carbon dioxide in the air has been steadily increasing again. This is due to humans burning fossil fuels and cutting down forests.

Early Earth   Earth today

Desert   Woodland

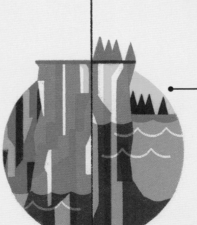

Low sea level   High sea level

SEA LEVEL
When Earth's climate gets warmer, water in the ocean expands. Ice in glaciers on land melts and the water flows into the oceans. This causes sea level to rise. Usually these changes happen over hundreds or thousands of years but because of global warming, sea levels are now rising much faster than normal.

IS EARTH OURS?

Humans as a species have only been present on Earth for a few million years. In that time our population has already reached over 7.8 billion, and it's still rising rapidly. We like to think of ourselves as the most dominant animal on the planet. In fact, there are many other life forms that have been around a lot longer and whose numbers make our population look small. So, is Earth really ours?

LIVING FOSSILS

Some living things have managed to survive even the worst mass extinction events. To do so, they have to adapt to all sorts of changes in the environment. These life forms are sometimes called living fossils because they have changed so little in such a long time.

Alive today   Fossils

HORSESHOE CRAB

One of the oldest life forms on the planet is the horseshoe crab. These ancient creatures have a thick protective shell and live on the seafloor, eating pretty much anything they can find. Their relatives first developed in the Ordovician period 485 million years ago, and modern forms can be traced back about 200 million years.

SHARKS

Sharks are a diverse group of fish, and their earliest examples developed over 400 million years ago. Because of habitat destruction and overfishing, some sharks are now in danger of extinction.

COCKROACHES

Cockroaches are some of Earth's most adaptive animals. They have been present on the planet for at least 300 million years.

SMALL BODIES, BIG NUMBERS

What ants lack in size, they more than make up for in numbers. With around 12,000 known species, ants can be found in a wide range of habitats on Earth. You can find them in rainforests, deserts, and everything in between. While getting an exact count is impossible, estimates for the total number of ants on the planet range from trillions to possibly 1 quadrillion (that's 1,000,000,000,000,000) individuals!

BACTERIA IN YOUR BODY

When it comes to big numbers of little life forms, bacteria take the top prize. Scientists estimate that a single adult human can have more than 38,000,000,000,000 (38 trillion) individual bacteria living in their body.

LIFE IN THE WATER

The oceans of the world are teeming with different life forms.

KRILL

Some of the most abundant creatures in the oceans are krill. Looking like tiny shrimp, krill are an important part of the ocean food chain and a favorite food of many whales. Current estimates say that there are about 500 trillion krill living in the world's oceans. Unfortunately, because of overfishing and pollution, their numbers are starting to decline.

TARDIGRADES

Among the most resilient—and strangest looking—creatures on the planet are tardigrades, also known as "water bears." These microscopic animals live in wet habitats all over the planet and can survive in subzero temperatures, in searing hot deserts, and even in outer space.

FISH

Fish come in many different shapes and sizes, from wriggly eels to streamlined ocean sailfish. All together scientists estimate that there are about 3.5 trillion (3,500,000,000,000) individual fish living in the oceans of the world.

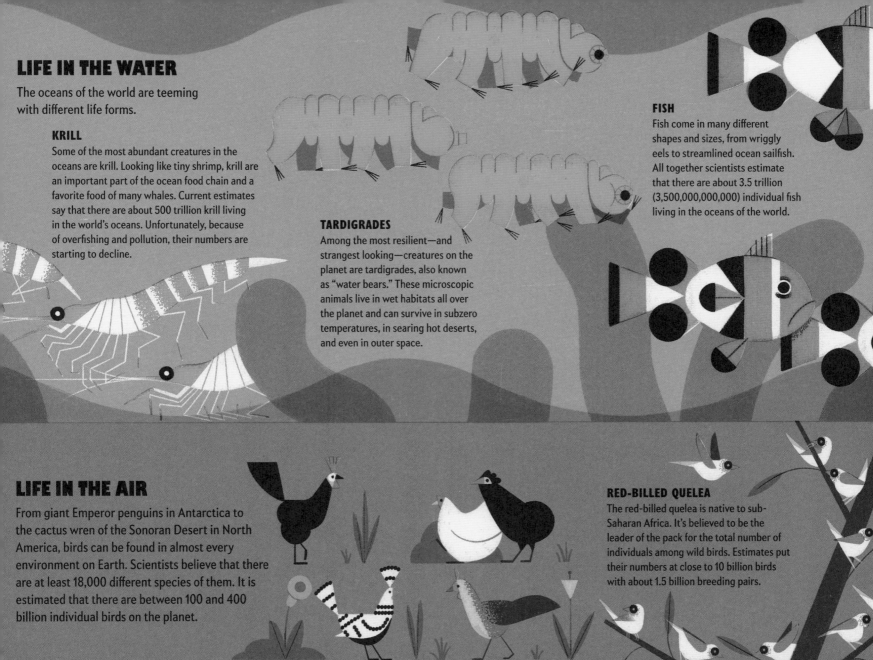

LIFE IN THE AIR

From giant Emperor penguins in Antarctica to the cactus wren of the Sonoran Desert in North America, birds can be found in almost every environment on Earth. Scientists believe that there are at least 18,000 different species of them. It is estimated that there are between 100 and 400 billion individual birds on the planet.

RED-BILLED QUELEA

The red-billed quelea is native to sub-Saharan Africa. It's believed to be the leader of the pack for the total number of individuals among wild birds. Estimates put their numbers at close to 10 billion birds with about 1.5 billion breeding pairs.

CHICKENS

When it comes to total numbers, there's one bird that stands tail and feather above the rest. Its scientific name is *Gallus domesticus*—but most of us just call them "chickens!" Current estimates say that there may be more than 50 billion of them on the planet.

MASS EXTINCTIONS

Over the last 600 million years or so there have been at least five major mass extinction events in which more than three-quarters of the life forms on Earth have suddenly died out.

Many scientists believe that we are currently in the middle of a sixth mass extinction, and humans are to blame because of the way we treat the planet. They believe that all of the animals pictured here went extinct at least in part because of human hunting. Today, a bigger danger for other species is humans polluting the air and destroying the natural habitats that plants and animals depend on. The burning of fossil fuels has had a big impact on Earth's climate too. The changing climate is making it impossible for some of our fellow Earthlings to survive.

Dodo

Mamo

Passenger pigeon

Columbian mammoth

Tasmanian wolf

EARTH IS UNIQUE

For thousands of years, people on Earth believed our planet was special because they thought it was the only planet with life. Over the past few decades, however, scientists have made lots of discoveries that suggest Earth may not be as unique as we thought. Even so, it's still our special home.

EXOPLANETS

In 1992, astronomers discovered the first confirmed exoplanets. These are planets that orbit a star outside of our solar system. Since then astronomers have identified more than 4,000 exoplanets orbiting other stars in our galaxy, and the number keeps growing every day.

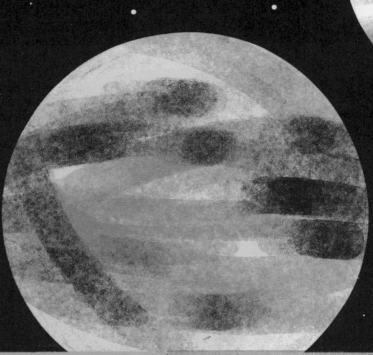

KEPLER-186F

Kepler-186f was the first Earth-sized exoplanet found in the habitable zone of a star. This is the region around the star where conditions are right for liquid water to form, just like on Earth. The discovery of Kepler-186f proved that there were other planets similar to Earth in the galaxy.

KEPLER-438B

Initial investigations have shown that this exoplanet is the most similar to Earth yet discovered. It's very similar in size, only about 12% bigger than our planet. Scientists can't be sure yet, but the temperature on the surface could be between 0 and 60°C (32–140°F). One big difference from Earth would be the length of a year—just 35 days on Kepler-438b. More recent studies have shown that the exoplanet's host star sends out regular "superflares." These emissions would probably make it too dangerous for life to develop.

ARE WE ALONE?

Back in 1961, astronomer Frank Drake was searching space for signals from other intelligent life forms. He wondered what the chance of finding another planet like Earth in the Milky Way galaxy was. To come up with a reasonable guess, he developed a mathematical formula that we now call the "Drake Equation." The equation starts with the number of stars in the Milky Way. Then it cuts that total down using different factors to work out how many planets there might be in the galaxy with life forms on them capable of communicating with us.

Astronomers now estimate that there may be 60 billion planets in the Milky Way with some type of life form on them. Only time will tell if some of them will give us a call!

SPACE INVADERS

Astronomers have recently discovered signs of complex organic molecules out in space in giant dust clouds. These are similar to some of the chemical building blocks that make up living cells on Earth. One idea about the origin of life suggests that it got its start from chemical compounds like these brought to Earth on meteorites, asteroids, and comets. This theory is called panspermia. In the past, the idea of the building blocks of life hitching a ride to our planet was pure science fiction. But there is growing evidence to suggest that it is a real possibility. And, if it happened here on Earth, it could have happened on other planets too.

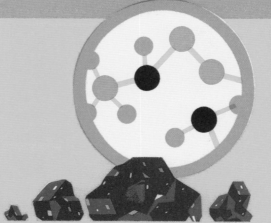

SUTTER'S MILL METEORITE

In April 2012, a carbonaceous chondrite meteorite struck northern California near Sutter's Mill. This is the same site that sparked the California Gold Rush of 1849. While this rock from space did not contain gold, when scientists analyzed it they found a number of complex organic molecules. These are chemicals commonly associated with simple life forms. This discovery provided more evidence for the idea that life on Earth may have gotten its start from objects in space.

EARTH—OUR SPECIAL HOME

Our planet is an incredible place. It's where we humans developed, and over hundreds of thousands of years we've adapted to living here in every environment. There may be other planets out in the universe with their own forms of life, or ones that would make a great home for humans in the future. But for now Earth is our home.

Unfortunately, Earth is under threat from pollution, climate change, and many other problems that could change it in ways that make it much less perfect for us. But there's still time to protect the planet, and there's lots you can do to help—from using less energy to getting on your bike instead of hopping in the car. Other ways to help include planting trees and recycling trash. It's up to all of us to protect our special home.

GLOSSARY

AXIS

A straight line that goes through an object, and which the object rotates around. Earth spins on an axis that passes through the North and South geographic poles.

ASTEROID

A rocky and metallic object in space that orbits the Sun and is smaller than a planet or dwarf planet. Most known asteroids are found in the asteroid belt between Mars and Jupiter.

BLACK HOLE

An object in space with a gravitational pull so massive that nothing, not even light, can escape. Because light can't escape, black holes appear totally black to observers.

BLUBBER

The thick fat of marine mammals such as whales and seals. The fat keeps them warm in the cold regions where many of them live.

COMET

An object in space made of ice and dust with a wide, oval shaped orbit around the Sun. Comets are most visible while close to the Sun, when they develop a long, bright tail of gas and dust as they melt.

CONDUCTOR

A material that allows heat or electricty to flow through it easily.

CONTINENTAL PLATE

One of the large pieces of Earth's crust that move slowly and independently on the surface.

CYANOBACTERIA

A group of bacteria that are able to create nutrients using sunlight through photosynthesis, like plants do. These single-celled organisms sometimes form colonies and are one of the oldest groups of living things.

DWARF PLANET

An object in space that orbits the Sun and is large enough to form itself into a round shape, but not large enough to clear out the other objects in its vicinity. One examples of a dwarf planet is Pluto.

ELECTROMAGNET

A temporary magnet created by wrapping a wire around a magnetic material (such as iron) and passing an electric current through the wire. Very powerful electromanets are used in industry and science.

EQUATOR

An imaginary circle around the middle of Earth that is the same distance from the North and South poles.

EXTINCTION

The process by which an entire species of living thing dies out.

FOSSIL FUEL

A fuel such as coal, petroleum or natural gas formed from remains of ancient animals and plants. Fossil fuels are burned to get energy.

GAS GIANT

A huge planet composed mainly of hydrogen and helium gases. The largest planets in the solar system, Jupiter and Saturn, are gas giants.

GLACIER

A large river of ice that is slowly traveling down a valley or mountain.

GOLDILOCKS ZONE

The area around a star where conditions are just right for liquid water to form. Many scientists think for a planet to show signs of life, it needs to be located in this "just right" zone.

ICE SHEET

A layer of ice that completely covers a wide area of land.

IGNEOUS ROCK

Rock formed when magma cools and hardens.

INVERTEBRATE

Any animal without a spinal column.

MASS

The amount of material in an object. How heavy an object is (its weight) depends on its mass and the force of gravity.

MATTER

The physical material that makes up objects in the universe, from the smallest particles to planets and stars. Matter has mass, while energy does not.

METAMORPHIC ROCK

A rock that has been changed by intense pressure or heat.

METEORITE

The rocky remains of an asteroid or comet found on the surface of Earth or another celestial object after crashing into it.

MINERAL

Naturally occurring solid materials that form rocks from which metals and other substances can be extracted.

MOLLUSK

A large group of mostly marine invertebrate animals. Most mollusks, including snails and clams, have external shells. However, some, such as octopuses and squids, do not.

MRI

Magnetic resonance imaging—a technique used by doctors to look at internal organs by aiming radio waves at a patient and studying the signals sent back.

NICKEL

A hard, silvery metal.

OCEAN LINER

A type of huge oceangoing ship that can carry thousands of passengers for several weeks at a time.

ORBIT

The route that one object takes around another, such as the Moon around Earth, or Earth around the Sun.

PALEONTOLOGIST

A scientist who studies fossils to learn about life long ago.

PRECIPITATION

Water falling from clouds to the ground as rain, snow, sleet, or hail.

PHOTOSYNTHESIS

A process where food is made using sunlight as energy. All plants produce at least some of their food through photosynthesis, as do some bacteria.

PRESSURE

A force applied on an object by another one it is touching.

SOLAR SYSTEM

The Sun and all the objects in space that orbit around it.

SUBLIMATION

The process by which a material changes from a solid into a gas, without becoming a liquid in between.

SUPERCONDUCTOR

A material that has no resistance (loses no energy) when electricty passes through it. Superconductors have to be kept very cold to function correctly.

SUPERMASSIVE BLACK HOLE

The largest type of black hole. Most galaxies have a supermassive black hole at their center.

TRILOBITE

Ancient group of invertebrate animals with a tough, exterior shell. Once among the most widespread animals, trilobites had entirely died out by the beginning of the Triassic period 252 million years ago.

VERTEBRATE

An animal with a spinal column. Vertebrate animal groups includes mammals, birds, fish, amphibians, and reptiles.

CONVERTING METRIC UNITS

In this book we've been using two systems of measurement, one called United States customary units and the other called the metric system. The metric system is used in nearly all science around the world, as well as being the most common system in everyday use in many countries. However, you might be familiar with other units.

United States customary units are the most common measurement units in use every day in the US. You probably know lots of these units, such as inches, feet, pounds, and gallons.

Below is a table showing how to convert the most common units from metric to United States customary units. If you're ever confused about a measurement in this book, take a look at this table.

LENGTH

1 millimeter (mm)	=	0.04 inches
1 meter (m)	=	3.28 feet
	=	1.09 yards
1 kilometer (km)	=	1,093 yards
	=	0.62 miles

VOLUME

1 liter	=	0.26 gallons
	=	1.05 quarts
	=	2.11 pints
1 cubic meter (m³)	=	264 gallons
1 cubic km (km³)	=	0.24 cubic miles

AREA

1 square meter (m²)	=	10.76 square feet
1 square kilometer (km²)	=	0.39 square miles
	=	247 acres

MASS

1 gram (g)	=	0.04 ounces
1 kilogram (kg)	=	35.27 ounces
	=	2.20 pounds
1 metric ton	=	1.10 tons

INDEX

SOURCE NOTES

Author's note

This book presents a wide range of information about our planet as well as many of the other objects in the universe. In order to make sure that the information is accurate and as up to date as possible, we've checked a variety of different sources and wherever possible we've used multiple sources to verify the same fact. The sources we used include books, articles from magazines and journals, and websites, many of which are listed below. Remember though that records are made to be broken and scientists are discovering new information everyday, so some of the facts presented here are bound to change! Finally, I would like to thank my son Stephen Tomecek, Jr. for his insight and for helping me develop some of the topics in this book.

Selected sources

American Museum of Natural Histroy (www.amnh.org)

Animal Diversity (animaldiversity.org)

Astronomy (astronomy.com)

Astronomy Notes (www.astronomynotes.com)

Atlas Obscura (www.atlasobscura.com)

Australian Antarctic Program (www.antarctica.gov.au)

Australian Museum (australian.museum)

Barkham, P. "The plight of Britain's ancient trees," *The Guardian* (www.theguardian.com)

BBC (www.bbc.co.uk)
    Bitesize (www.bbc.co.uk/bitesize)

Birding World (birding-world.com)

British Heritage (britishheritage.com)

Calculator Soup (www.calculatorsoup.com)

Cells Alive (www.cellsalive.com)

CERN (home.cern)

ClearlyExplained.com (clearlyexplained.com)

Cool Antarctica (www.coolantarctica.com)

Cool Math (www.coolmath.com)

Davies, E. "The world's largest spider is the size of a dinner plate," *BBC* (www.bbc.co.uk)

Discovering Antarctica (discoveringantarctica.org.uk)

DK Find Out (www.dkfindout.com)

EarthSky (earthsky.org)

Enchanted Learning (www.enchantedlearning.com)

Engineering Toolbox (www.engineeringtoolbox.com)

Engineer's Edge (www.engineersedge.com)

ESA (www.esa.int)

Science & Technology (sci.esa.int)

Geology (geology.com)

Ghosh, P. "Modern humans left Africa much earlier," *BBC* (www.bbc.co.uk)

The Guardian (www.theguardian.com)

Guinness World Records (www.guinnessworldrecords.com)

Health Line (www.healthline.com)

Herbert Nitsch (www.herbertnitsch.com)

Hewings-Martin, Y. "How many cells are in the human body?", *Medical News Today* (www.medicalnewstoday.com)

History.com (www.history.com)

How Stuff Works (www.howstuffworks.com)

Hubble Site (hubblesite.org)

IFL Science (www.iflscience.com)

Info Please (www.infoplease.com)

Jabr, F. "It's Time to Face Facts, America: Masks Work," *Wired* (www.wired.com)

Kids Health (kidshealth.org)

Lakritz, T. "12 of the longest flight routes in the world," *Insider* (www.insider.com)

Library of Medicine (www.ncbi.nlm.nih.gov)

Live Science (www.livescience.com)

Live Strong (www.livestrong.com)

Lumen Learning (courses.lumenlearning.com)

Marine Mammal Center (www.marinemammalcenter.org)

Marshall, M. "First land plants plunged Earth into ice age," *New Scientist* (www.newscientist.com)

Mining (www.mining.com)

Mining Tech (www.mining-technology.com)

Nace, T. "'It's Almost Like Another Planet' ¬¬– Coldest Temperature On Earth Recorded In Antarctica," *Forbes* (www.forbes.com)

NASA (www.nasa.gov)
    Imagine the Universe! (imagine.gsfc.nasa.gov)
    Solar System Exploration (solarsystem.nasa.gov)
    SpacePlace (spaceplace.nasa.gov)
    Space Science Data Coordinated Archive (nssdc.gsfc.nasa.gov)

National Geographic (www.nationalgeographic.com)

National Geographic Kids (www.natgeokids.com)

National Oceanic and Atmospheric Administration (www.noaa.gov)

Science On a Sphere (sos.noaa.gov)

Natural History Museum (www.nhm.ac.uk)

Nature (www.nature.com)

NHS (www.nhs.uk)
       NHS Inform (www.nhsinform.scot)

Nine Planets (nineplanets.org)

Oldest (www.oldest.org)

OneKindPlanet (onekindplanet.org)

Open University (www.open.edu)

Pennisi, E. "A surprisingly simple explanation for the shape of bird eggs," *Science* (www.sciencemag.com)

Periodic Table (periodictable.com)

Phys.org (phys.org)

Planet Facts (planetfacts.org)

Princeton (www.princeton.edu)

Reference (www.reference.com)

RSC (www.rsc.org)

RSPB (www.rspb.org)

Sample, I. "Kepler 438b: Most Earth-like planet ever discovered could be home for alien life," *The Guardian* (www.theguardian.com)

San Diego Zoo (animals.sandiegozoo.org)

Sciencing (sciencing.com)

Science.org (www.science.org.au)

Science Learn (ww.sciencelearn.org.nz)

Science Focus (www.sciencefocus.com)

Science Notes (sciencenotes.org)

Science World (www.scienceworld.ca)

Scientific American (www.scientificamerican.com)

Shark Trust (www.sharktrust.org)

Sizescom (www.sizes.com)

Sky At Night Magazine (www.skyatnightmagazine.com)

Smithsonian Magazine (www.smithsonianmag.com)

Space.com (www.space.com)

Speed of Animals (www.speedofanimals.com)

Statista (www.statista.com)

TheSkyLive.com (theskylive.com)

Thought Co (www.thoughtco.com)

Track Spikes (trackspikes.co.uk)

Universe Today (www.universetoday.com)

U.S. Geological Survey (www.usgs.gov)

Water Encyclopedia (www.waterencyclopedia.com)

Weather.gov (www.weather.gov)

Web Elements (www.webelements.com)

Weight of Stuff (weightofstuff.com)

Wei-Haas, M. "Why does Earth have a moon, and how does it affect our planet?," *National Geographic* (www.nationalgeographic.co.uk)

Whale Facts (www.whalefacts.org)

WHO (www.who.int)

Wildlife Sense (wildlifesense.com)

World Atlas (www.worldatlas.com)

World Life Expectancy (www.worldlifeexpectancy.com)

Wunderground (www.wunderground.com)

WWF (www.worldwildlife.org)

Yosemite (www.yosemite.com)

Zielinksi, S. "George the Lobster Should Stay in Maine Waters," *Smithsonian Magazine* (www.smithsonianmag.com)

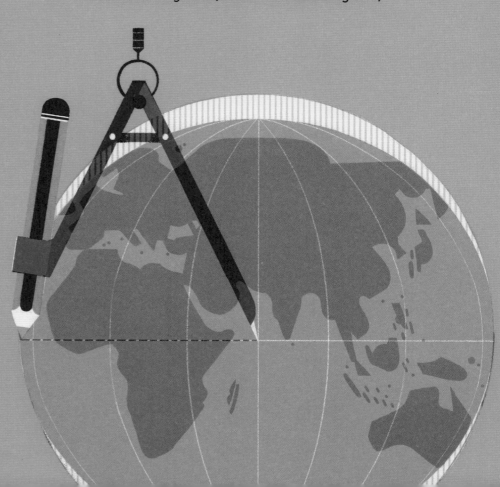

*This book is dedicated to all those individuals
working to make our planet a healthier, safer, and
more welcoming place for all of Earth's inhabitants—
May You Live Long and Prosper!*

STEVE TOMECEK

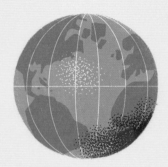

What on Earth Books is an imprint of What on Earth Publishing
Allington Castle, Maidstone, Kent ME16 0NB, United Kingdom
30 Ridge Road Unit B, Greenbelt, Maryland, 20770, United States
First published in the United States in 2021

Text copyright © 2021 Stephen M. Tomecek
Illustrations copyright © 2021 Marcos Farina

Staff for this book: Patrick Skipworth, Editor; Andy Forshaw, Art Director

ISBN: 978-1-9129203-4-1

Printed in China

1 3 5 7 9 10 8 6 4 2

whatonearthbooks.com